THE PHOTOGRAPHER AND THE LAW

THE PHOTOGRAPHER
AND THE LAW

Don Cassell

Consultant Editor: Richard Gordon, MA, LL.M,
Barrister-at-law

BFP BOOKS London

British Library Cataloguing in Publication Data

Cassell, Donald
  The photographer and the law.—2nd ed
  1. Photography. Law.
  I. Title
  342.4'97

ISBN 0-907297-19-6

First Published 1984

New Edition 1989

Published by BFP Books (Lyndtree Ltd), Focus House, 497 Green Lanes, London N13 4BP, and printed in Great Britain by BPCC Wheatons Ltd., Exeter.

Acknowledgements

Since the first edition of this book was published in 1984 there have been a number of major changes in the law which will have far reaching consequences for both professional and amateur photographers.

Undoubtedly the most dramatic change is in the law of copyright and in this respect I am indebted greatly to solicitor Roy Furness who has edited the chapters on this complex subject.

Richard Gordon, barrister-at-law, edited the first edition with the exception of the chapters on copyright and although he has not been able to edit the revisions, I remain indebted to him for his help and advice on the first edition.

As far as the revisions are concerned I would like to record my thanks to Walter Greenwood, co-author of *Essential Law for Journalists*, for his help in those parts dealing with the Criminal Justice Act 1988, the Police and Criminal Evidence Act 1984 and the Official Secrets Bill.

My thanks are also due to the publishers for bringing out this second edition of the book.

Contents

Preface

This book is written for all photographers, and in writing it I have tried to bring together the many strands of the law which affect the photographer, whether he or she be professional or amateur.

It will come as a surprise to many readers, I suspect, to realise how often in following their photographic profession or hobby they can fall foul of both the civil and criminal law. Of course, all of us in our everyday life can do likewise, but it is no exaggeration to say that photographers may be much more at risk in certain circumstances.

Photographers—especially those employed in the news media—are often more at risk of being manhandled and having equipment damaged. How many photographers are aware of their rights under the law in these circumstances? This book points out these rights and discusses the remedies available.

Many photographers lack knowledge of consumer law as it affects their hobby or profession. Consequently, part of this book is devoted to outlining rights which every citizen has under what has now become popularly known as consumer law.

It must be stressed that this is not a "do it yourself" law book. It is said that a lawyer who represents himself has a fool for a client, and the aim of the book is simply to explain the law in readily understandable language.

Neither is the book a substitute for legal advice should it be necessary. I hope that the book will serve a dual purpose: firstly, to help photographers steer clear of legal pitfalls, and secondly, to inform them of their rights.

With rights, however, come responsibilities towards others, and it is just as important that photographers should be aware of the duty owed to those they may come across in following their hobby or profession.

There are references in the book to various offences which carry fines and/or imprisonment. Recently it has become the practice for Parliament to agree that fines be increased to keep pace with inflation, and rather than having to amend every piece of legislation which carries financial penalties, offences have been grouped together in bands or categories so that one or all of the categories can be increased as and when it is thought necessary by Parliament, without having to introduce enabling legislation for each individual offence.

For this reason, as far as possible maximum fines are not mentioned in this book.

Donald Cassell

CHAPTER ONE

The Meaning and Scope
of Copyright

To understand the concept of copyright it is useful to trace its historical background, for so often in the mists of times long past are the first principles of today's laws to be found.

In medieval days, education was confined to the privileged few, many of whom were clerics. As education, such as it was, spread, more persons became able to write and even translate books from their original language into English.

Those who had the ability to write and publish books banded together to form the Stationers Company, and the first concept of copyright appeared in 1533 when the company was granted protection against the importation of foreign books. In 1556 Queen Mary granted the Stationers Company the right to seek out and destroy books printed in contravention of the earlier statute.

Even today, under the Copyright, Designs and Patents Act 1988, the owner of copyright has the right to apply to the Court to seize copies which infringe that copyright.

Mary, of course, had ulterior motives in granting the charter to the Stationers Company. She was, perhaps, more concerned to control the religious opposition to her reign and by strengthening what was virtually a monopoly held by the Stationers Company, she was creating what was to become copyright; looked at from a simplistic point of view, all copyright is a legally backed monopoly to protect a person's intellectual property.

What Mary in effect created was a licence to publish, and for a book to be lawfully published it had to be entered in the register of the Stationers Company. In the turbulent years that followed Mary, it paid Elizabeth and the subsequent Stuart kings to uphold such a licensing system as an effective way of controlling opposition in the form of the written word.

However, it was inevitable that, as the strength and power of Parliament increased at the expense of the monarchy, Parliament, in 1694, refused to renew the licence the Stationers Company had held for 160 years.

To protect the intellectual property of writers, the first Copyright Act was passed in 1709, followed by a further Act in 1814. In 1842 another Copyright Act repealed all previous Copyright Acts and became the governing statute for literary copyright until the 1911 Act.

Meanwhile, engravings, sculptures and musical and dramatic performing rights had become protected by further legislation. During this period the Fine Arts Copyright Act was passed in 1862 and this brought paintings, drawings and photographs within the realm of copyright which protected intellectual property for the life of the author plus seven years.

The Copyright Act 1911 extended copyright to the typographical format of published editions. This Act was superseded by the Copyright Act 1956 which, in turn, is now superseded by the Copyright, Designs and Patents Act 1988 which, for the sake of brevity, will be referred to as the CDPA.

Prior to these Acts, however, there had been a number of decided cases in which the concepts and labour of the person's creation was upheld.

One of the main concepts of copyright has been that of originality, and in 1890 there was a landmark judgment in the case of *Palgrave's Golden Treasury of Verse*, a compendium of poetry gathered together from the work of many poets which was first published in 1861, and has been updated and published constantly since that date.

The *Golden Treasury* had been protected by compilation copyright and the issue before the court was that of originality. The court held:

"In cases of work not original in the proper sense of the term but composed of, or compiled or prepared from materials which are open to all, the fact that one man has produced such a work does not take away from anyone else the right to produce another work of the same kind and in doing so use all the materials open to him".

What is a photograph?

It is worth noting at this stage that the CDPA in Section 4(1)(a) defines "artistic work" as, among other things: "a graphic work, photograph, sculpture or collage, irrespective of artistic quality". Section 4(2) says:

"Photograph means a recording of light or other radiation on any medium on which an image is produced or from which an image may by any means be produced, and which is not part of a film".

This is a rather more precise definition than that which appeared in the 1956 Act and which was generally considered to be unsatisfactory as far as photographers were concerned. Bodies representing both amateur and professional photographers expressed dissatisfaction in evidence presented to a Government appointed committee under Mr. Justice Whitford which was set up in 1973 "to consider and report whether any, and if so what, changes are desirable in the law relating to copyright as provided in particular by the Copyright Act 1956 . . .".

In their representations to the committee, photographic bodies expressed the view that the definition of a photograph should be amended to exclude reprography, on the basis that photocopies produced automatically by a machine were not original but the result of a mechanical process and did not warrant copyright protection as photographs.

The new definition may or may not meet these objections. Photocopying machines do, of course, make copies on paper by means of the transmission or recording of light on paper. It is also worth noting that the phrase, "irrespective of artistic quality", which was in the old Act, is repeated in the new legislation.

This is an important phrase because a photograph can be appalling, it can be out of focus, over or under exposed and have no artistic merit whatsoever, yet still be protected by copyright. This underlines the basic theory of copyright, the protection of a person's creation however poor that creation may be.

It was because of this that the Whitford Committee, when it reported in

1977, commented on the suggestion of photographic bodies as far as reprography was concerned, that this would introduce a standard of artistic merit which would be a new departure in copyright law and which, if it was carried further, might have implications in other fields.

The Whitford Committee also turned down a suggestion that the definition of a photograph should no longer exclude a cinematograph film, a distinction first introduced in the 1956 Act, and the committee could see no reason for putting back the clock.

This view has obviously been underlined in the CDPA even though the word "cinematograph" has been dropped. The use of the word film in the definition under the CDPA must be taken to refer to a cinematograph film or video tape.

The scope of copyright

So what is, and is not, subject to copyright? Section 4(1)(b) and (c) includes in the definition of artistic work a work of architecture, being a building or a model for a building, or a work of artistic craftsmanship.

The definition of a photograph has already been stated, but because photographers so often photograph inanimate objects they ought to know what is meant by the phrase "artistic craftsmanship". The new legislation does not define what is meant by artistic craftsmanship but Section 4(2) says that graphic work includes any painting, drawing, diagram, map, chart or plan and any engraving, etching, lithograph, woodcut or similar work.

Sculpture includes a cast or model made for the purpose of a sculpture.

It is interesting to note that the Act does not define collage, which is described in the *Concise Oxford Dictionary* as an abstract form of art in which photographs, pieces of paper, matchsticks, etc., are placed in juxtaposition and glued to the pictorial surface. It may be argued that as far as the CDPA is concerned a collage, like beauty, is in the eye of the beholder!

It is important for photographers to realise the extent to which copyright applies to visual objects, for so many photographs are taken of inanimate visual studies and artistic works and in many cases the photographer is in ignorance of the copyright situation.

Therefore, for the sake of clarity what can best be described as other people's copyright will be considered first. The CDPA sets out what can be done in relation to copyright work without an infringement of copyright. Section 31(1) states that copyright in a work is not infringed by its incidental inclusion in, inter alia, an artistic work, film or cable programme.

Consequently, a photographer taking a general shot which might have a copyright object in the background is unlikely to fall foul of copyright law because the inclusion of such material would no doubt be held to be incidental. But what of a photographer who makes a collage of, say, photographs of famous models and then photographs and publishes the finished result? It can hardly be argued in any sense that the inclusion of those photographs—always provided they are covered by copyright—is incidental inclusion.

Copyright in an artistic work is not infringed by it being copied in the course of instruction or of preparation for instruction, provided the copying is done by a person giving or receiving instruction and it is not by means of a reprographic process.

Public buildings, monuments and statues

Copyright which exists in buildings, models for buildings, sculptures and works of artistic craftsmanship is *not* infringed by photographing them when they are permanently situated in a public place or in premises open to the public.

This is the situation which obtained under the 1956 Act and is a common sense point of view because, as we have seen, copyright exists to protect intellectual property and to allow the owner of such copyright to exploit it. The taking of photographs of buildings and works in a public place is not going to prevent the architect or designer from exploiting his work.

The Whitford Committee was critical of the phrase "premises open to the public" because they considered it to be of uncertain meaning. Nevertheless, the phrase is repeated in Section 62(1)(b) of the CDPA.

Consequently pieces of sculpture and works of artistic craftsmanship on temporary display in public galleries may well be protected by copyright, but Section 62 of the new Act does allow what might otherwise be termed breaches of copyright, such as photography for private use.

Architecture

As far as architecture is concerned, copyright in plans and drawings, or in models for a building, belongs to the architect unless he is employed when, as in other cases of an artistic work by an employed person, the copyright belongs to the employer unless there is an agreement to the contrary.

Such copyright continues to run for 50 years after the death of the architect, but as Section 62 of the CDPA says: "However the copyright in a building is not infringed if it is painted, drawn, photographed or filmed."

Paintings and drawings

With paintings and drawings, copyright belongs to the artist and continues until 50 years after his or her death. The artist keeps the copyright even if the picture has been commissioned and it cannot be reproduced without the artist's permission.

Engravings, etchings, lithographs, woodcuts or similar works are also protected by copyright which would belong to the creator of the work or their employer, so photographs of these subjects should not be taken without the consent of the copyright holder, which is only likely to be withheld if the photographs are being taken for commercial purposes.

Old masters would, of course, be out of copyright. While these can be photographed, the problem for photographers is one of either gaining access to them or obtaining permission to take pictures of them from the current owners, and this topic is dealt with in Chapter 9.

Everyday objects and handicrafts

There are a host of everyday objects which a photographer, for a variety of reasons, may wish to capture on film. Many of these are taken for granted but may be subject to the provisions of the new Act.

Part III of the CDPA states that a design right is a property right which exists in the design of any shape or configuration of the whole or part of an article. But under Part IV of the Act designs, which are registrable, mean features of shape, configuration, pattern or ornament applied by any industrial process and which are of aesthetic value.

Although copyright would be unlikely to exist in a can or a bottle the design for such may be registrable under the new Act, and an original design continues to be protected for 15 years from the end of the calendar year in which it was first recorded in a design document or an article was first made to the design, whichever first occurred.

On the other hand, items of gold or silverware, jewellery, fabric, glassware, porcelain and pottery are all subject to copyright and as we have seen earlier in this chapter, would be protected—for a period of 50 years—as a work of artistic craftsmanship.

Obviously to make an exact copy of an article in the same material would be a breach of copyright. A photographer taking pictures of such items might well be held to be in breach of copyright, especially if the photographs were used for commercial purposes, but photographs of mass produced articles are unlikely to produce problems as far as copyright is concerned.

A photographer wishing to take photographs of an item of artistic craftsmanship should make simple inquiries about its provenance. If this leads to the photographer discovering that the article is subject to copyright and he wishes to photograph it—especially if this should be for commercial use—then he should take the precaution of seeking the consent of the copyright owner.

Common sense would seem to dictate that consent is unlikely to be refused. A photograph taken for commercial use is likely to increase the demand for the particular item or ones similar to it. As one of the objects of the law of copyright is to protect the intellectual or artistic work of the creator and to enable them to exploit it commercially, it would be ironic if permission was refused.

Entertainment and performances

There are other aspects of copyright, the breaching of which may result in trouble for a photographer, and this can be dealt with under the heading of entertainment.

It is not uncommon for newspapers and magazines to publish photographs or a strip of photographs, taken from a television screen. This is a breach of copyright, but usually the television company concerned is quite happy to give permission for the material to be used provided an acknowledgement is printed alongside the picture or pictures. This acknowledgement usually takes the form of a one line attribution acknowledging the source such as "Picture(s) by courtesy of BBC TV" (or Thames TV or whatever company owns the copyright).

Stage shows, operas, ballets, concerts, etc., are also protected by copyright, but where photography is concerned it is only necessary to look at copyright as far as it affects capturing on a still photograph extracts from a performance. One photograph is unlikely to be considered to be a breach of copyright, which exists not only in the words and/or music, but in the costumes, stage design and the way it is presented.

In short it can be said that copyright exists in almost anything that has been produced as a result of a person's skill, labour and judgment. There is even copyright in a football fixture list which, although hardly a literary work, is a result of skill and labour on the part of the compiler.

Exceptions to copyright

There are exceptions to copyright: there is no copyright in an idea or in news. Consequently any item in the news or something which would fall into the category of current affairs can be photographed without fear of breaching copyright.

Of course copyright does exist in the way in which a newspaper or magazine reports an item of news, for this involves skill on the part of the journalist who wrote the particular item.

However a word of warning must be entered here: frequently court cases make news headlines, but there are other restrictions concerning photographs as far as court and crime stories are concerned and these will be dealt with in later chapters.

Neither is there copyright in a person's appearance. Anyone in a public place or who can be seen from a public place cannot legally object if their photograph is taken, but always be aware of the dangers of using a photograph in a manner which could be libellous. This is dealt with in Chapter 3.

However there are some primitive tribes who shun having their photographs taken as they fear that the taking of a photograph will spirit away their soul, thus precluding themselves from enjoying whatever life after death their religion promises them! And only recently, while on holiday in West Africa, the author discovered that despite the fact they were devout Muslims there are still some West Africans who pay for a ju-ju which they wear to protect themselves from being photographed!

A further word of caution would not be out of place at this point. Although there is nothing to stop a photographer from taking anyone's photograph, as will be apparent from later chapters the photographer may be guilty of a nuisance. However much would depend upon the circumstances of the individual case.

As there is no copyright in ideas, there is nothing to stop a photographer from hiring a model used by Patrick Lichfield or David Bailey and using the same pose and location. Although the photographer would rightly be accused of plaigiarism, he has used his own skill and labour in taking the photograph.

The situation would be different, however, if the photographer tried to pass off the pictures as having been taken by Lichfield or Bailey.

Photographic copyright

The new Act makes one very important change in the law as far as copyright of photographs is concerned. Under the new legislation, copyright in a photograph will expire not, as under the old law, 50 years after first publication, but at the end of the period of 50 years from the end of the calendar year in which the author dies.

The only exception to this is if the work is of unknown authorship, when copyright expires at the end of the period of 50 years from the end of the calendar year in which the work is first made available to the public.

The new Act has introduced this concept of "unknown authorship", which is defined as applicable where the author is unknown and it is not possible to ascertain his or her identity by making reasonable inquiry.

This could apply to photographs, for it is not unknown for a collection of photographs taken long ago to come to light with the identity of the photographer or photographers being unknown and unascertainable.

Quite often these photographs are of value for a number of reasons apart from any artistic merit they may have. Copyright in these photographs will last for 50 years from the end of the calendar year in which they are first made available to the public, which in the case of photographs—which come under the heading of artistic work—includes when first exhibited in public.

The copyright position of old photographs is now as follows:

Photographs taken before 1st June 1957 will continue to be protected by copyright for 50 years from the year in which they were taken;

Photographs taken since 1st June 1957 and until the commencement of the new legislation will be protected by copyright under the old legislation for 50 years from the year of first publication.

There are many famous photographs which are out of copyright and have been so for many years, some of which have been compiled to demonstrate the development of photography and the skills of photographers. The manner in which they are displayed in such a book would be protected by compilation copyright, for even though the photographs are not original, skill and labour have been involved in the compilation.

Although, as already noted, there is no copyright in ideas, copyright does protect a person's original work and it is worth noting briefly what is meant by "original". In *Kilvington Brothers Limited v Goldberg* (1957), a Canadian case, Mr. Justice Judson held that novelty and inventiveness were not necessarily the test of originality. He held—and it must be remembered that the case he was trying concerned the design of a tombstone and not a photograph—that to be original it must be the original expression of the thoughts of its creator.

On the surface this may well seem to contradict the statement that there is no copyright in ideas, but the acid test would be the question of skill and labour involved.

How, also, would this apply to the imitation of a Lichfield or Bailey photograph? Again, the acid test is the question of skill and labour and these criteria would be met by the photographer hiring the model and seeking out the same location, as well as posing the model in the same way and physically taking the photograph.

Also, it might be difficult to adjudicate on whether or not the same idea was conceived by one photographer at the same time as it was by another, or even by a third or more.

CHAPTER TWO

Copyright for photographers

Having examined the theory of copyright and those areas in which it exists as far as photographs are concerned, it is now necessary to look at who owns the copyright of photographs. Section 1(1) of the CDPA states that copyright exists in, inter alia, artistic works which—as noted in the previous chapter—includes photographs.

Section 154(1) of the legislation states that work qualifies for copyright protection if the author was at the material time—

(a) a British citizen, a British Dependent Territories citizen, a British National (Overseas), a British Overseas citizen, a British subject or a British protected person within the meaning of the British Nationality Act 1981, or
(b) an individual domiciled or resident in the United Kingdom or another country to which the relevant provisions of this part extend, or
(c) a body incorporated under the law of a part of the United Kingdom or of another country to which the relevant provisions of this part extend.

The reference "to which . . . this part extend" means that Parliament may extend the provisions of copyright protection as far as publication in this country is concerned to Commonwealth or foreign countries which, in many cases, are likely to be signatories to international copyright conventions. By the same token a photograph first published in a country to which this part of the Act extends would also have its copyright protected in this country. In fact, there are few parts of the world to which international copyright conventions do not apply.

A body corporate is usually a commercial concern established and incorporated under the laws of the United Kingdom or another country to which the copyright protection provisions extend.

Photographers in employment

The new Act makes two radical changes as far as photographs are concerned. The first affects photographers in employment.

Under the old law, if a photographer was employed by the proprietor of a newspaper, magazine or similar periodical under a contract of service or apprenticeship and the photograph was taken for publication in that periodical, copyright belonged to the proprietor "insofar as it relates to publication in any newspaper, etc., or reproduction of the work for the purpose of its being so published."

In all other respects the photographer was entitled to copyright remaining in the work.

Also under the old 1956 Act, however, in the case of non-press work, where a photograph was taken in the course of the photographer's employment by another person, under a contract of service or apprenticeship, that other person was entitled to any copyright subsisting in the work.

Section 11(2) of the CDPA states:

"Where a literary, dramatic, musical or artistic work is made by an employee in the course of his employment, his employer is the first owner of any copyright in the work subject to any agreement to the contrary".

It will be noticed that this section does not have the subsidiary clause for press workers reserving copyright for other uses to the photographer.

Naturally the derogation of the right contained in the old 1956 Copyright Act was vigorously challenged by such interested bodies as the National Union of Journalists and by many members of both Houses of Parliament, but to no avail.

The only way in which a photographer can reserve to himself what might be called subsidiary rights, is if such an agreement is included in the contract of service.

Commissioned photography

The other major change was in commissioned photography. Under the old law the person who commissioned a photograph was the owner of the copyright, and this was frequently a bone of contention.

Representations were made to the Whitford Committee by the Royal Photographic Society and the Institute of Incorporated Photographers (now the British Institute of Professional Photography) that copyright should be held by the photographer and not the person who commissioned the photograph.

They also suggested that the photographer was not necessarily the person who actually operated the mechanism which released the camera shutter; rather, it should be the person responsible for organising the photography.

Although the Whitford Committee felt such a definition lacked certainty, it nevertheless recommended that the author should be defined as the person responsible for the composition of the photograph.

In the CDPA the only attempt to define authorship as far as photography is concerned is in Section 9(1) which says the author, in relation to a work, means the person who creates it.

Nevertheless, professional photographers will welcome the fact that there is no suggestion in the new Act that the person commissioning the photograph will own the copyright unless the contrary is agreed.

It is considered unlikely that the person commissioning a photograph would demand that they become copyright owners. Nevertheless, cases such as *Williams v Settle (1960)* can still arise for photographs not covered by the new legislation.

In this case a photographer was commissioned to take a photograph of the plaintiff's wedding. Two years later the plaintiff's father-in-law was murdered.

The dead man appeared in the wedding photograph and the photographer sold copies to some national newspapers. In the subsequent action it was held that copyright belonged to the plaintiff (the bridegroom) and not the photographer.

The position would have been different had the photographer taken the wedding pictures "on spec", even if he sold copies of the group photograph, as there would have been no commissioning of the photographs.

As a result of the new legislation *Williams v Settle* could still apply, but in reverse. If the photographer holds the copyright, there would be a breach of his rights if the subject or a member of the wedding group sold a picture for publication.

If a photographer does agree that the copyright should be the property of the person commissioning the work, he should consider a number of important factors and have them included in the commissioning agreement which, in the photographer's own interests, *should* be in writing.

At the time of the Whitford Committee, the Committee on Photographic Copyright which represented nine major organisations covering all aspects of photography, said the following should be considered when considering the fee to be charged on executing a commission:

How will the photographs be reproduced/shown?
For what purpose will the work be reproduced?
How long (time period) will the work be reproduced/published/sold?
What is the print run—how many copies will be made?
In what geographical areas will the work be reproduced/published?
How many editions/impressions/versions are to be published?

These are points which any photographer considering passing the copyright to the commissioner should ask, for upon the answers must depend the size of the fee charged.

Ownership of negatives

There is one vexed question not really answered by the new Act, and that is the age old one of who owns the negatives.

It has been the custom for many, many years for professional photographers to claim ownership of the negatives in the case of commissioned work. This claim is one I have never been happy with, for to the best of my knowledge it had no foundation in law. Indeed, where a photographer charges a customer for the film as well as developing and printing, I can see no legal grounds for the photographer refusing to hand over the negatives.

After all, the customer has paid for the film and the developing of it and there is no reason, in my mind, why the application of chemicals to a film to change them into negatives for which the customer has paid, should give the photographer the right of ownership. The only certain way round this is for photographers to ensure that they buy their own film and do not charge the client directly for it. This way the photographer retains ownership of the material and the subsequent negatives.

Obviously, under the new legislation photographers will usually own the negatives anyway, along with copyright. However, photographers who do contract to part with copyright whilst also charging the client for the film used, should really consider handing the negatives over as part of the deal and simply increase their basic labour charge to compensate, as happens in the case of colour transparency work where it has always been the custom to pass the slides to the client and charge accordingly.

Copyright protection

There are certain steps all photographers should take in protecting the copyright of their photographs. In all cases each print or slide should bear the name and address of the photographer prefaced by the statement "Copyright of . . .", and the year in which the photograph was created. Although there is no need for the photograph to bear the International Copyright symbol © there is no harm in it doing so.

A photographer who takes a dramatic news picture should always be careful of any agreement he signs with a news and/or picture gathering organisation. While many national newspapers and many television companies, as well as leading agencies, are prepared to pay a substantial sum for a dramatic and exclusive picture, they will almost inevitably want to either purchase the copyright outright or have exclusive overseas rights.

The reason for this is that it gives the particular purchaser the opportunity of recouping the money paid for the photograph. The photographer who finds himself in this position should read carefully any agreement he signs, and be absolutely certain of all or any rights he is signing away.

To give some indication of the position, the magazine *Practical Photography* asked what the *Daily Mirror* picture desk would offer for a hypothetical picture of someone diving into the Thames to save a royal corgi from drowning while the Queen looked on aghast.

After getting over his amusement the deputy picture editor told *Practical Photography*:

"Well first of all I'd want to make damn sure that he hadn't already offered it to any other papers. It's quite common practice for photographers to try auctioning a picture by phoning one or two of the other nationals and then phoning us and saying, 'Well so and so offered so much' hoping we'll make a better offer.

"No, if it was a really good picture, sharp with clear faces and well composed, I'd get a team and editor down right away. You have to have an editor for negotiations if a picture's likely to be worth more than about £2,000, and we'd want to make very sure that the photographer had copyright.

"I'd say we'd start talking around £5,000 to £10,000 for that hypothetical picture. Then you'd have to come to some agreement about world syndication rights. This is usually worked on a 60/40% basis with 60% going to the photographer.

"But if he was prepared to sell us the rights they would probably be worth another £10,000 or so. It depends on a whole number of factors really".

That summarises the type of deal a photographer can make with a world beating photograph. If the photographer owns the copyright, what he receives for the picture is based on its current worth and how shrewdly he can bargain. It is during the bargaining process that the photographer must reach his own decision about what rights he is legally going to assign to a newspaper. This is a decision he must make for himself; in an ideal world he should seek legal advice, but since time is likely to rule this out he must be very aware of what rights he is selling. It is no use a disgruntled photographer complaining after the event that he signed away his rights, for, unless fraud or duress was involved, the law will not intervene.

Assignment of copyright

Because copyright exists to protect the author, under which description a photographer falls, it follows that when he is the copyright holder he may do what he wishes with this right. He may sell it, if he can find a buyer, or he can give it away to whomsoever he chooses, and that person or persons then takes over all the rights which accrue to the copyright holder.

Copyright is a property right which can be sub-divided into three main areas which are:

1. As to the nature of the right, for example, film rights, broadcasting rights, etc.;
2. As to the territory where the rights apply, for example, Britain, Europe, Commonwealth, etc.;
3. The period for which it is to operate.

In effect this means that a photographer may, for example, assign his rights in a photograph for publication in the USA for a period of ten years, at the end of which time copyright for that area reverts to the photographer.

But in order to have the right identified, Section 28 provides that the author must assert that right.

Assignment has to be in writing or by operation of law. This means that copyright can be left in a will to a particular person or body, and if a photographer died intestate the copyright would pass to whoever is entitled to it under the law governing intestacy.

For the copyright holder who is unfortunate enough to become bankrupt, copyright vests in the receiver for the benefit of creditors. Similarly, any body corporate which goes into liquidation would find any copyright it held applied to reduce any debts.

Some years ago it was not unknown for some magazines to accept a photograph for publication and when paying for its use endorse on the back of the cheque the following, or similar words:

"Cashing this cheque will be taken as passing the copyright in the photograph for which this cheque is payment to . . .", with the name of the publishing company.

This practice has now almost died out but some cases still arise from time to time. By cashing the cheque the photographer need not fear losing the copyright. Copyright cannot be passed by the method described above, and photographers who find themselves in such a situation should simply strike out the endorsement on the back of the cheque and write "I do not agree" or similar words on it.

As will be noted from this and the previous chapter, copyright can be a complicated subject and any photographer who feels he or she has had their copyright infringed should seek legal advice as soon as possible.

Moral rights

As a result of the new Act the concept of "Moral Rights" has been introduced, which gives a photographer the right to be identified whenever the work is published commercially or exhibited in public, or a visual image of it is broadcast or included in a cable programme service. It also covers the case where a film showing a visual image of the work is shown in public or copies of such a film are issued to the public. However, Section 78 requires that this right must be asserted in writing.

Exceptions are when the photographer is employed and the photograph is taken as part of their employment, for any work made for the purpose of reporting current events, or where it is published in a newspaper, magazine or similar periodical, or in an encyclopaedia, dictionary, yearbook or other collective work of reference, and is made for, or made available with the consent of the author for, the purpose of such publication.

Nor does it apply to Crown or Parliamentary copyright or a work in which copyright originally vested in an international organisation.

A person who has their moral rights infringed has the right to sue for breach of statutory duty owed to them.

Moral rights are not assignable, but the right to identification as the author of a photograph or to object to derogatory treatment of the author's work may be bequeathed in a will. In the event of the photographer dying intestate, the moral right, which only applies to the author and not the copyright owner unless, of course, they are one and the same, continues to subsist until twenty years after a person's death, and the right is exercisable by the photographer's personal representatives.

False attribution

Apart from the moral right to have their work acknowledged, except in those circumstances already discussed, Section 84 gives photographers the right not to have work falsely attributed to them. This situation could arise if a photograph is published or exhibited with the name of a photographer who did not take the picture given as the author. Under Section 86(2) the right continues to subsist until 20 years after a person's death.

It is difficult to conceive of circumstances, other than for a fraudulent purpose, where the name of a leading photographer would be given as the author of a photograph that he did not take, although of course there could be circumstances when a photographer is wrongly named by mistake. False attribution would also apply if anyone sought to possess or deal in a photograph in the course of business, using the name of a photographer who was not the author of them.

The right not to have false attribution of a photograph exists even after the death of the person to whom a photograph has been falsely attributed.

As far as "doctoring" a photograph is concerned, the photographer whose photograph has been treated in this manner may seek an injunction—which a court may grant if it considers it an adequate remedy in the circumstances—which will prohibit "doctoring" a photograph unless a disclaimer is made, in such terms and in such manner as may be approved by the court, disassociating the photographer from this treatment of the work.

Rights to privacy

Section 85(1) of the Act states that: A person who for private and domestic purposes commissions the taking of a photograph or making of a film . . . has the right not to have (a) copies issued to the public; (b) copies exhibited or shown to the public; (c) copies broadcast or included in a cable programme.

Since this right applies to a photograph or film taken for private or domestic purposes, it is arguable that a wedding group would fall into that category. This section would therefore apply to situations such as the *Williams v Settle* case, where a photographer who has the copyright of a photograph taken as the result of a commission seeks to publish it at a later date without permission.

The section refers specifically to a photograph being issued to the public, or exhibited or shown in public, and this raises a number of interesting points.

Would shown in public cover publication in a newspaper? A photograph published in a newspaper, if it does not come within the meaning of "shown in public", must surely be covered by the term "issued to the public".

But there is also a more intriguing point to be considered, especially by commercial photographers who exhibit portfolios, portraits, etc., in shop windows. Common sense dictates that this must come under the definition of exhibiting or showing in public, and it is reasonable to assume that inclusion of similar photographs in a promotional brochure would also be exhibiting to the public, albeit a restricted section.

Photographers may, however, seek the protection of Section 87 of the Act, which does not make it unlawful to exhibit or display photographs taken for private and domestic purposes if consent has been given. Wedding and portrait photographers in particular should bear this important point in mind when accepting a photographic commission. The most effective way that a photographer can ensure that problems do not result from displaying or exhibiting commissioned photographs, is by getting the commissioner to waive their rights in writing.

Such permission, unless a contrary intention is expressed, made in favour of the owner or prospective owner of the copyright, is presumed to extend to his licensees and successors.

Copyright infringement

Even the mere copying of a photograph is what the Act describes as "an act restricted by copyright" unless the copier has the permission of the copyright holder. It is even a breach of copyright to include a photograph which is protected by copyright in a broadcast (television) programme or in a cable programme.

The new legislation deals in depth with what is described as secondary infringement of copyright, and infringing copies. This can best be described as possessing in the course of a business, selling or offering for sale, letting or offering to let for hire, a work protected by copyright, or distributing the work otherwise than in the course of a business, to such an extent as to affect prejudicially the rights of the copyright owner.

On the other hand fair dealing—of which the Act does not offer an explanation as to what would constitute fair, or indeed unfair dealing—in a photographic work for the purpose of research or private study does not infringe copyright.

Fair dealing with a work for the purpose of criticism or review would not infringe copyright provided that it is accompanied by sufficient acknowledgement as to the identity of the copyright owner.

What, then, would be the position of a newspaper or magazine if it wished to review a collection of photographs and reproduce one or more as part of that review?

The question of whether a substantial number are reproduced is quite distinct from fair dealing. It is only when the Court has determined that a substantial part has been taken that the question of whether or not this constitutes fair dealing will arise.

However, once this question has arisen, the degree of substantiality—that is to say, the quantity and value of photographs taken—becomes an important factor in determining whether there has been fair dealing. As in all aspects of the law, there can be no hard and fast rule: each case must depend on its own particular facts.

It should be noted that the use of a photograph for the reporting of current events is not fair dealing under Section 30(2) of the new Act. Although the use of other copyright works for the purpose of reporting current events is not an infringement if sufficient credit is given, in the case of photographs the copyright owner's permission must be sought.

Certain exceptions are also made for the use of copyright work being copied for educational purposes, providing such copying is done by the person giving or receiving instruction and is not done by means of a reprographic process.

Neither is copyright infringed by anything done for the purpose of Parliamentary or judicial proceedings or proceedings of a Royal Commission or statutory inquiry.

Remedies for infringement

Infringement of copyright is actionable on the part of the copyright owner, to whom a number of remedies are open. The copyright owner can seek damages, an injunction restraining future breaches of copyright, an account of profit made as a result of the copyright breach or other remedy as would be available for the breach of any other property right.

Section 97 of the Act provides that in an action for infringement if it is shown that at the time of the infringement the defendant did not know, and had no reason to believe, that copyright subsisted in the work, the plaintiff is not entitled to damages. Nevertheless in such circumstances the plaintiff can enforce any other remedy available to him.

The Act also enables a court, having regard to all the circumstances and with particular reference to the flagrancy of the infringement and any benefit received by the defendant as a result of the infringement, award "such additional damages as the justice of the case may require".

Section 99 gives the copyright owner the right to order an offender to deliver up photographs that are in breach of copyright, while Section 114 provides for the forfeiture and destruction of offending photographs, etc., with the right of the Court to consider the adequacy of other available remedies.

Obviously, it is to be hoped that a court would take into consideration the ability of a person in breach of copyright to actually pay any damages awarded if this is to be considered an alternative to a forfeiture order.

There is also criminal liability in the Act for making for sale or hire, importing into the United Kingdom other than for private or domestic use, or possessing in the course of a business with a view to committing an act infringing the copyright, an article which is, and which the person knows or has reason to believe is, an infringing copy of a copyright work. Section 107 also imposes criminal liability where there is a prejudicial effect on the copyright owner if a person distributes otherwise than in the course of a business an infringing article.

This section is unlikely to affect any but the top photographers, whose work might well be pirated and sold by unscrupulous people as an original.

Photographic competitions

Photographic competitions are becoming increasingly popular and high standards of photographic initiative, imagination and quality are revealed as a result of such competitions.

Any photographer entering such a competition must, for his or her own protection, read and understand the rules of the competition. To begin with, many of them state that entries will only be returned if stamped addressed envelopes are sent with photographs or transparencies.

Also among the conditions of entry may be acceptance of a disclaimer by the promoter of the competition from liability for loss or damage. Thus the photographer is on notice that, if there is loss or damage, he has no claim against the promoter or organiser for he has voluntarily accepted the risk.

Such competitions even have as a condition that prize-winning entries may be used for publication, promotional or advertising purposes, and that the copyright passes to the publication or promoter.

By signing such an entry form, which is more than likely to state that the entrant has read and agreed to be bound by the conditions of entry, one is, in effect, assigning copyright. The photographer must therefore consider whether or not the prizes on offer are worth the loss of copyright.

One must take a common sense point of view and the photographer must ask this question:

"If my entry is of sufficiently high a standard to win a prize, could I benefit more if I did not enter, retained my copyright and tried to get better value by selling the photograph elsewhere?"

Again, common sense would seem to dictate that the answer may be no, for photographic competitions which offer good prizes may well be based on a particular theme—leisure is one prime example—in which only the promoter has an interest, and entering the competition may be the only chance the photographer has of realising the value of a particular photograph.

However, to be avoided are those competitions—happily few these days—where the rules state that copyright in *all entries* passes to the organisers. By this method the organisers are obtaining the copyrights in perhaps hundreds of original pictures, yet only a select handful of prizewinners receive any award. The vast majority of entrants will have given their copyright away for nothing.

Photographic agencies

Gifted amateur photographers as well as professionals frequently lodge the results of their work with photographic agencies who in turn provide transparencies to newspapers, magazines, advertising agencies or anyone requiring a particular shot.

For many photographers this is a useful way of trying to make money from their pictures without the trouble of having to find outlets for its publication themselves.

Picture agencies do a good job but it must be remembered that their primary aim is to make money for themselves. It is therefore essential for any photographer to fully understand what the terms or conditions of business of such agencies are.

Who owns the copyright? What fee will the agency pay each time the picture is used? When are fees paid and for how long does the agency have sole right to use the picture?

These are all questions which have to be asked and to which answers satisfactory to the individual photographer received. But above all else it is essential that the terms and conditions of the agency are read and understood by the photographer.

Readers will know that the law expects people to enter into contracts being fully aware of what is involved, and it's no use saying at a later date "I didn't trouble to read the terms or conditions" or "I didn't understand them", if anything goes wrong.

International copyright conventions

Finally, there is the question of international copyright conventions to be considered. In past years there have been a number of treaties between this country and other countries which provide copyright protection outside the British Isles.

There is the Berne Convention which goes back to 1886 and has been the subject of a number of revisions, the last being in Paris in 1971. The changes made in the Paris convention, mainly of a minor nature, have not yet been ratified by this country except for administrative clauses, and would involve changes in the existing law.

The only change to have any bearing on photographers is that of moral right, the inalienable right of a photographer to claim authorship, etc. which has already been discussed.

As far as this country is concerned it is the revision of the convention held in Stockholm in 1967 which is the latest applicable. The convention provides that authors will receive the same protection in other countries which are signatories to the agreement as they do in their own country.

The length of the protection in one country cannot be greater than that existing in the country of origin of the particular work.

The other international convention is the Universal Copyright Convention 1952, which brought the United States of America into an international copyright agreement. Under this particular convention, unless the contrary is specifically stated, a country must provide the same copyright treatment to citizens of subscribing countries as it gives to its own.

It also sets out minimum standards of protection which, in the case of a photograph, is ten years.

Model release forms

Although not within the scope of the copyright law this is an appropriate place to deal with model release forms.

Strictly speaking such a form isn't necessary in law; there is no copyright in a person's body and copyright belongs to the photographer, especially when he has paid the model. However, a model release form serves a more than useful purpose as far as use of the photographs is concerned.

Depending on the wording of the model release form, the photographs can be put to any legitimate use, without the model having a comeback unless, of course, accompanying material or a caption libels the model.

They can be used for publication in any form including advertising. A model release form can also serve as a receipt and will obviate any dispute over whether or not the fee has been paid, and even the amount.

It is best for the form to be signed at the end of a modelling session, as the model will then be perfectly aware of the type of pictures which have been taken. If a model under 18 has been used, the release should be signed by a parent or guardian.

If the model is working through an agency, the agency can sign on the model's behalf, and this signature is as legally binding as if the model had signed the form personally.

It should be noted that although release forms are valuable for the above reasons and should always be used wherever possible, a model's refusal to sign at the end of a session does not necessarily mean that the photographer is then unable to make use of the pictures. Unless copyright has been passed to the model, he or she has no legal grounds for preventing subsequent publication of the photographs.

Although one is perfectly at liberty to take pictures of the public at large, it can also be useful to get release forms signed even in these circumstances, where one or more people appear prominently in a picture. This is particularly the case if there is any chance that the pictures may subsequently be placed with a picture agency that may sell rights for advertising use, or for travel brochures and similar publicity material.

CHAPTER THREE

Libel

It is frequently said that a camera cannot lie: As far as this refers to the capturing on film of a person, object or incident, it is undoubtedly true, but photographs in conjunction with captions have been, and probably will continue to be, the subject of libel actions.

Libel is part of the law of defamation, which exists to protect the professional and private, that is moral, reputation of a person from an unjustified attack, and covers the spoken and written word. The spoken word, slander, can be conveniently omitted because a photograph is classified with the written word as being in permanent form, whereas the spoken word is transient. (Although not relevant, untrue oral statements made on television or radio are classified as libellous rather than slanderous as is, under the Theatres Act 1968, a public performance of a play).

To succeed in a libel action the plaintiff has to prove three points:

(1) The words refer to the plaintiff;
(2) They were published in permanent form; and,
(3) They were defamatory or capable of bearing a defamatory meaning.

Defamation

So what is defamatory? Unfortunately there is no all-embracing definition of defamation as far as the law is concerned. What is defamatory today may not be considered defamatory tomorrow. Twenty years ago, to describe someone as "gay" meant that person was, to quote a dictionary definition, "lively, merry, light-hearted, cheerful, bright. . . . " Today it would also be necessary to add "homosexual". And again much would depend upon the manner in which the word was used. To say of a person: "He's always light-hearted and smiling and gay" might or might not be considered to be a defamatory use of the word "gay". But to describe someone as "a gay" or even "gay" when that person was not homosexual, could well be libellous.

In today's society, where people are far more tolerant about homosexuality than they were twenty or thirty years ago, and homosexuality being a fact of life, it might not even be held to be defamatory to describe someone as "gay".

The first satisfactory definition of what is defamatory was that of Baron Parke in *Parmiter v Coupland (1840)*, who held that a publication calculated to injure the reputation of another by exposing him to "hatred, contempt or ridicule" was defamatory.

Many years later—84 to be exact—the deficiency of this definition was recognised, and in *Tournier v National Provincial and Union Bank of England,* Lord Justice Atkin observed: " . . . but it is obvious that suggestions might be made very injurious to a man's character in business which would not, in the ordinary sense, excite hate, ridicule or contempt; for example, an imputation of a clever fraud which, however much to be condemned morally and legally, might not yet excite what a member of the jury might understand as hatred or contempt".

Next came a further definition which at first sight seemed strange. In the last days of the Czarist Empire in Russia, the monk Rasputin rose to prominence in the court. In the early 1930s, MGM Pictures Ltd made a film in which it was suggested that Princess Youssoupoff had been either seduced or raped by Rasputin.

The princess, who was then living in exile in Paris, sued for libel, and MGM were unable to prove that she had, in fact, been either seduced or ravished by Rasputin. Now it would appear that to have been seduced or raped is unlikely to expose a person to hatred, ridicule or contempt but Lord Justice Slessor in the Court of Appeal made the following points: " . . . as has been frequently pointed out in libel, not only is the matter defamatory if it brings the plaintiff into hatred, ridicule or contempt by reason of some moral discredit on her part, but also if it tends to make the plaintiff be shunned and avoided and that without any moral discredit on her part".

In an uncertain world one thing is certain, that the law does not stand still. It is constantly changing and finding remedies for injuries for which none existed hitherto. Libel is no exception, so it is not surprising to find that the definition of what is defamatory was extended yet again, this time in the case of *Sim v Stretch (1936)*.

It was Lord Atkin, by this time a Lord of Appeal in Ordinary, in a House of Lords judgement, who was again critical of the definition of Baron Parke, and a further test evolved: Would the words complained of tend to lower the plaintiff in the estimation of right thinking members of society?

Over the years there have been a number of libel actions which were brought because of allegations which had been made about the competence or otherwise of a particular person, which has led to what can be called an omnibus definition: that the words complained of disparaged the person in his office, profession or trade.

Thus we have four definitions of what constitutes a defamatory statement. They are a statement, or statements, which:

1. Expose a person to hatred, ridicule or contempt;
2. Cause him to be shunned or avoided;
3. Lower him in the estimation of right thinking members of society generally; and,
4. Disparage him in his office, trade or profession.

The conditions for libel

As has already been noted, what can be held to be defamatory can change over the years. Most trials for libel are heard by a judge and jury. It is for the judge to decide whether the words complained of are capable of bearing a defamatory meaning, and for the jury to decide whether or not they were defamatory. If the judge decides the words are not capable of bearing a defamatory meaning, that is the end of the case.

To succeed in a libel action the plaintiff also has to prove the libel was published, and referred to him. As far as books, magazines and newspapers are concerned, publication is presumed.

As publication must be to a third person, there can be no libel in showing offending material to the person concerned although criminal libel could be a possibility. But a photograph which might, because of its caption, be libellous, would be published if shown to a third person.

This raises an interesting point as far as photographers are concerned: if it was possible for a photograph to be libellous per se, would handing it to a commercial firm of developers and printers constitute publication? There is no doubt that the handing in of a telegram, or the posting of an envelope or a postcard containing libellous material, constitutes publication to a third person.

Today many films are developed and printed mechanically, and it is possible that a potentially libellous photograph could be developed and printed without ever being seen by human eyes. However it is the practice for processing companies to check prints for correct colour register, etc., among other technical purposes, and this would constitute publication.

What is important is that the person bringing a libel action is either identified by name, or if unnamed, is capable of being identified by a person or persons known to him.

Innuendo

It is therefore possible to have a situation where a photograph and caption can be libellous without the person portrayed being named.

To understand why, it is necessary to look at the question of what libel lawyers refer to as the innuendo, or hidden meaning. Innuendo derives from the Latin word meaning to nod or to hint at, and is frequently pleaded by a plaintiff when words complained of as being libellous are not defamatory in themselves. They become defamatory by reasons of their conjunction with another statement, or because of some extrinsic circumstance or fact.

Two cases which illustrate the meaning of innuendo when linked with a photograph are *Cassidy v Daily Mirror (1929)* and *Tolley v Fry (1931)*. In Cassidy's case a race horse owner named Michael Cassidy was attending racing at Aintree with a lady.

A *Daily Mirror* photographer asked to take a picture of Cassidy and the lady, and it appeared with the following caption: "Mr Michael Cassidy and Miss . . . whose engagement has been announced".

Unfortunately for the *Daily Mirror*, Mr Cassidy was married but separated from his wife, who brought an action for libel. She pleaded the innuendo in the caption that those who knew her as Mrs Cassidy would think she was living a lie, and that she was not in fact Mr Cassidy's wife but his mistress with whom he was living. Mrs Cassidy was awarded £500 damages.

Another fine example of the use of an illustration which, combined with words, resulted in a libel action, was Tolley's case.

Tolley was a well known amateur golfer, and Fry the makers of chocolate. They published a caricature of Tolley with a packet of Fry's chocolate sticking out of his rear pocket, and a verse extolling the virtues of the chocolate. In the subsequent libel action Tolley successfully claimed that the innuendo was that he had prostituted his amateur status, as it was thought he had consented to, and been paid for, the advertisement.

It can be seen how careful those who work with illustrations and photographs have to be to avoid actions for defamation.

Care with locations

Even the taking of photographs of nude models on location can lead to a libel action. There is a case which was settled out of court involving a well known British glamour magazine. A nude model was posed on a motor launch. There was nothing exceptional about the photograph. Unfortunately, the name of the boat was clearly visible and its owner alleged that people who knew him from his boat would believe that he was in the habit of allowing nude girls to disport themselves on it.

Presumably the photographer involved did not obtain a release from the boat owner for its use for glamour photography, and this is a point all photographers should bear in mind. There are some beautiful old houses and similar places in the country which make superb locations for glamour photography. There is no harm in using them provided the owner consents and is fully conversant with what use the house or grounds will be put to. Without that consent the photographer is not only trespassing but laying himself open to a possible action for libel.

Care with captions

The dangers which a caption to a photograph can provide if the facts contained in the words are inaccurate or give rise to an innuendo, have been referred to, and the photographer has a positive duty to ensure the facts are correct. It is very common in the provincial press, trade publications and some magazines, for group photographs to be taken at social functions, when people are captured on film with glasses in their hand.

The obvious caption to such a photograph would be:

"A group of friends enjoying a drink at such and such occasion".

On the surface there is no harm in that: unfortunately, one, or perhaps more than one, member of that group may be known for having strong views on alcohol and be a teetotaller. The liquid in the glass that particular person is holding may be a tonic or a sparkling mineral water. To a photographer it looks like a gin or vodka and tonic. Once that photograph and caption is published the teetotaller is in a very good position to bring an action for libel.

It would not be difficult for that person to prove he or she had been ridiculed or held in contempt on the ground of hypocritical behaviour, of holding himself or herself out as a teetotaller and then to be described as "enjoying a drink".

It could be argued that the phrase "enjoying a drink" was justified on the grounds that the particular person was enjoying a drink, one which was non-alcoholic. That is undoubtedly true, but the phrase "enjoying a drink" is used almost exclusively with reference to alcohol. So in the illustration cited there would be the innuendo that the teetotaller was drinking alcohol.

In most, if not all, cases of libel in which photographs have been involved, it is the innuendo which has caused trouble. There are a number of well known campaigners against pornography, some of whom have in fact carried out research in Soho strip clubs, and photographs of them doing so have appeared in the media with an explanatory caption or accompanying story.

But if one of those persons was pictured entering a cinema which showed soft porn films and it was published without any caption, the innuendo would be clear: that person was a hypocrite, for the assumption would be that he or she was visiting such an establishment for pleasure. It would be almost impossible for a newspaper or magazine to prove the contrary.

Another source of danger from use of photographs is found in stock or library pictures to illustrate newspaper or magazine features. Among past cases was an action brought by a Smithfield meat porter against a national daily newspaper.

In this case the photograph was used as an illustration to an article on pilfering from Smithfield Market. The porter claimed that the innuendo was clear: he was guilty of stealing meat. He received a sum of money in damages.

So too did a girl model whose photograph was taken from stock and used to promote a product as being good for expectant mothers. Unfortunately for the advertising agency which created the advertisement, the girl was not an expectant mother, neither was she married. Again damages were paid.

Unintentional defamation

In many of the cases cited there would now be a defence provided by the Defamation Act 1952—that of unintentional defamation. Prior to the passing of the Act it was no defence to an action for libel to claim that it happened unintentionally or accidentally. As far as the law was concerned it was not the intention or lack of intention which mattered. The mere fact that a person had been libelled was sufficient.

Hence the case of *Cassidy v Daily Mirror*. The photographer in that case had no intention of libelling Mrs Cassidy; indeed neither he or the newspaper could have had any knowledge of the existence of the wife, otherwise the picture and caption would not have been published.

The Defamation Act has provided a way for an unintentional libel to be settled by a newspaper or magazine without litigation which, in defamation actions, can be costly.

The defence of unintentional defamation relies on two points:

1. The words (i.e. caption) complained of were published innocently;
2. An offer of amends is made in accordance with the Act.

As far as innocent publication is concerned, it has to be shown that the publisher did not intend the words to refer to the plaintiff and knew of no circumstances by virtue of which they might be understood to refer to him, or the words were not defamatory on the face of them and that he (the publisher) knew of no circumstances by virtue of which they might be defamatory of the plaintiff.

The publisher also has to undertake, as the offer of amends, to publish a suitable correction and what is described as a "sufficient apology" to the aggrieved person.

There are other technical provisions which need not be explored. It is sufficient to say that most experts believe *Cassidy's* case would fall within this defence. But what of the example cited above? If a paper published the photograph and caption of the teetotaller "enjoying a drink" would that constitute innocent publication?

Much would depend on the circumstances: if the photographer (and it is necessary to presume he wrote the caption) did not know the aggrieved person was a teetotaller, it is likely that the defence of unintentional defamation would succeed.

On the other hand if the photographer knew the aggrieved person was a teetotaller, the defence would obviously fail and damages would certainly be heavier.

Exhibitions

So far the discussion has concerned publications as far as the Defamation Act is concerned. Would it apply to unintentional defamation committed during an exhibition of photographic work? Section 4(1) commences: "A person who has published words alleged to be defamatory of another person ... "

Although generally thought of as an Act which applies to the media, with the exception of Section 7 which deals with the qualified privilege of newspapers, and the two parts of the schedule which lists newspaper statements having qualified privilege, there is nothing in the Act to suggest it applies exclusively to newspapers. Indeed, it is described as "an Act to amend the law relating to libel and slander and other malicious falsehoods".

Publish is defined in dictionaries as "to make generally known; to proclaim; to print and issue for sale, books, music, etc".

Consequently it would seem to be logical to suggest that an exhibition would be covered by the Act, although whether or not a suitable correction and sufficient apology (as required by the Act if the defence of unintentional defamation was raised) placed in a prominent place in the exhibition would be sufficient to the aggrieved person, is an interesting point to consider.

Doctored photographs

A great source of danger is the doctoring of photographs, either by use of an airbrush to paint out part of a photograph, creating a montage, or other means of altering the visual picture depicted.

There is an old Fleet Street story, which may or may not be apocryphal, of the Press Lord who was showing his wife the layout and pictures for the following day's paper, a paper which, incidentally, had a great appeal to "genteel" ladies. One of the pictures to be published was that of a prize bull.

It wasn't the bull that horrified the Press Lord's wife, but that part of his anatomy which would make the bull in demand for breeding. She insisted that this was something which would horrify the "genteel" lady readers, and her husband ordered the offending organ to be painted out.

It was with the result, so the story goes, that legal action followed, the owner of the bull claiming he had been made to look ridiculous by the emasculation of his animal.

The story may not be true, but it is an amusing and instructive example of the dangers which can result from painting out part of a picture, or even cropping one to excise a person or persons. Most doctoring is not done deliberately; there may be good technical reasons for touching up or painting out part of a picture, but in doing so, the greatest care must be shown to ensure no one is inadvertently libelled.

It is very easy to doctor a photograph and put the head of a well known politician or personality onto another person to produce a satirical effect, which may be strengthened by a caption.

There are circumstances when such a doctored photograph holds a person up to ridicule or disparages him in his office, trade or profession. Most of the butts of this type of doctored photograph are politicians who, fortunately for the publications concerned, take this in their stride and accept it as part of the price to be paid for being in the public eye. Nevertheless, it should be remembered that there could come a time when a particular politician or personality decides that a doctored photograph and/or caption has gone too far, and a writ for libel is issued. It will then be interesting to see what that particular individual's reputation is worth in terms of monetary damages.

Candid photography

Candid camera shots may well present the greatest risk of libel. By their very definition such photographs show people in amusing (to others), embarrassing and, often, humiliating situations, and there is an element of risk as far as libel is concerned. Great care should be taken to obtain a release from the "victim" of such photographs if it is to be published. Such a release constitutes consent, and consent is a complete defence to a libel action.

There is one other risk in taking candid camera photographs, and that is of criminal libel, although prosecutions for the offence are rare.

Criminal libel

Unlike libel in a civil action, where publication to a third person has to be proved, in a prosecution for criminal libel it is only necessary to prove publication to the person libelled. Furthermore, a person accused of criminal libel has to prove not only the truth of the libel but that publication was for the public benefit.

The reason for what is an onerous duty placed on a defendant to prove that publication was for the public benefit, and the reason why there is an offence of criminal libel, is because publication might lead to a breach of the peace or seriously affect the reputation of the person libelled.

One of the most famous cases of criminal libel in recent years was that brought by Sir James Goldsmith against *Private Eye*, who told magistrates hearing the committal proceedings: "When a campaign of villification takes place the repercussions can sometimes lead to a breach of the peace".

However under Section 8 the Law of Libel Amendment Act 1888, it is necessary for a High Court judge to give permission for a prosecution for criminal libel against a newspaper. It appears that in the *Private Eye* case the judge who granted permission accepted it was not essential to prove the likelihood of a breach of the peace occurring.

The *Private Eye* case did not come to trial; the parties came to terms and Sir James withdrew the prosecution. If the person who published the criminal libel knew it to be false he may be fined or imprisoned for up to two years, although if he did not know the libel was false the term of imprisonment is reduced to a maximum of one year.

In all past cases involving criminal libel it has been the publication of words which has led to the prosecution. In a Court of Criminal Appeal judgement in *R v Wicks* (*1936*) the point was made as follows: "... words written of a man which are likely to provoke him to commit a breach of the peace, or, if seen by others, to hold him up to hatred, ridicule or contempt or damage his reputation".

It does not take much imagination to see how a candid camera shot linked with a caption could do just that.

There is another category of libel, that of obscene libel, which is rarely, if ever, heard of today, doubtless because of the Obscene Publications Acts 1959 and 1964 which will be dealt with in a later chapter.

Defences to libel actions

A brief reference has been made to defences available in an action for libel, and reference made to the Defamation Act 1952 which provided the useful defence of unintentional defamation. As was mentioned, this would apply to *Cassidy's* case, and could well apply to what can be described as "caption libels".

By this is meant that it is the caption or comment accompanying the photograph which is libellous, and the care which must be taken when writing captions has been mentioned, especially in connection with the example of a group photograph where one person said to be enjoying a drink was a teetotaller.

There are other defences available which will be briefly mentioned, but before doing so, it must be noted that action for libel has to be brought within three years of publication of the offending material, and is a personal action in the eyes of the law.

All this really means is that the action dies with the person libelled, so the death of a plaintiff in a libel action brings an end to the action, unlike other actions for damages which may continue after death for the benefit of the dead person's estate.

The reason why a libel action dies with the plaintiff should be obvious: not being alive the plaintiff is unable to care about his reputation. It could be argued that the dead person's reputation matters to his loved ones, especially if the libel complained of was particularly bad, and many might consider that an action should continue if only to vindicate the dead plaintiff's reputation.

Of course if the plaintiff agreed to the publication that, too, is a complete bar to an action for libel, and this underlines the necessity of getting a release from those who figure in candid camera shots. It will be remembered that one of the dangers which could face a photographer and publisher of such shots, is that of innuendo.

The example of a prominent anti-pornography campaigner entering a Soho sex shop or strip club has been cited. Similarly, the fact that a person enters a public house is not by itself pejorative, but if that same person was pictured staggering out of licensed premises, to many people there would be a clear innuendo that that person was, to say the least, the worse for drink.

But he or she might not be: they could be feeling faint or have tripped over a piece of torn floor covering, or caught their heel or have been the victim of other mishaps which caused them to stagger, and may not have taken a drink at all.

It is in these situations and in candid camera shots, where a person is put in a ridiculous position, that an innuendo can arise. Hence the importance of obtaining consent to publish such a picture, and this should be obtained in writing using words which are precise and very much to the point.

The purpose of publication should be included as should, if possible, any caption which is to be used, because as has been demonstrated in the last chapter, it is the flip or carelessly written caption which leads to so much trouble as far as libel is concerned.

Another defence is that the libel has already been adjudged. All this really means is that the case has already been heard and disposed of one way or the other, and no action can be brought against those responsible for publication of the libel.

But to go back to the example of the teetotaller said to be enjoying a drink. That person could have brought a libel action which could have been settled out of court, and as far as the first publication of picture and caption is concerned the matter has ended.

There the matter should end, because the competent picture libararian would have removed the offending caption and fixed a note to the picture explaining the libel which was contained in the caption. Normally this precaution would be sufficient, but life has a perverse habit of distributing banana skins for the unwary and if by any chance there was cause to use the picture again, and the warning note had come away and it was published with a similar offending caption, there would be a fresh cause for a libel action.

It would be no use pleading that the case had already been adjudged; it had, for the publication of the original libel. But every subsequent publication of the libel is a fresh publication and consequently a new libel.

This fact demonstrates that care must be taken when filing pictures over which there has been the slightest hint of trouble. It is far better to destroy picture and caption than risk a future libel action.

Justification and fair comment

Justification, with one exception, is a complete defence to a libel action, but as far as a photograph is concerned it could never apply to one which had been doctored. To prove justification it is necessary to show the words complained of are true in substance and in fact; substitute the word photograph for words and it can clearly be seen how the defence must fail with a doctored photograph.

However the libel is most likely to be committed in a caption, which again demonstrates how the greatest care must be taken when writing caption, comment, or what-have-you to accompany a photograph for publication either in print or at an exhibition.

There is a further point to be kept in mind when considering the defence of justification: that is that not only must the words complained of be justified, so too must any innuendo.

The exception to the rule that truth is a complete defence against an action for libel is to be found in the Rehabilitation of Offenders Act 1974. This act laid down that a convicted criminal who has served a sentence of no more than thirty months imprisonment will, after ten years, be rehabilitated. The actual amount of time which must pass before a person can claim to be rehabilitated as far as a conviction is concerned, and can then claim that it is spent, depends on the severity of the sentence.

But if a spent conviction is revealed and the defence of justification raised, this defence can be negated if malice on the part of the publisher can be proved. Once again it shows how care must be taken with captions.

Another defence which is much used by publications is that of fair comment, and needless to say, this defence can only be used if words which accompanied a photograph by way of a caption were libellous. To succeed in the defence of fair comment it is necessary to show that the matter complained of was, indeed, fair comment made in good faith without malice and in the public interest. It is also necessary that the facts upon which the comment was made were true.

It is not necessary to convince a jury that the comment was one which would be held by a reasonable man. It can be unreasonable, but if it can be proved it was the honestly held opinion of the writer, without malice, and that the facts on which the comment was based were true, there is a defence.

The defence of privilege, or absolute privilege as it is commonly known, applies only to reports of judicial proceedings in the United Kingdom. The defence of qualified privilege could conceivably be raised in connection with a photographic libel, but it is difficult to envisage this in the case of a photograph published without a caption.

Finally, the defence of accord and satisfaction has to be considered. The essence of this defence is that the alleged libel has been disposed of, and this is not to be confused with the defence that the matter has been previously adjudged.

The libel could have been disposed of if the plaintiff has accepted publication of an apology and correction as satisfactory. Such apology and correction may well be accompanied by a sum of money paid to the plaintiff, or into court if a writ for libel has been issued.

However it is necessary to sound a warning: great care should be taken when phrasing an apology and correction to make sure a fresh libel is not perpetrated or the actual libel admitted. It is in circumstances such as these, as in all cases of defamation, when it is essential to take legal advice as soon as possible.

CHAPTER FOUR

Obscenity

"Dirty pictures" are almost as old as the camera itself, and the expression conjures up pedlars in Oriental bazaars or the seedy back street bookshops of Soho and other major cities.

In recent years the frontiers of what can be published have been expanded at almost breathtaking speed. Prior to and during the Second World War, quality magazines like *Lilliput* and *Men Only* had discreetly posed photographs of nude female models which revealed little and left a lot to the imagination.

Today all that has changed; everything is revealed and nothing left to the imagination. Photographs in certain magazines depict couples or groups in simulated sex and almost anything goes. From time to time magazines are seized by police and either made the subject of a destruction order or, occasionally, a prosecution is brought under the Obscene Publications Act 1959, which codified and put into statute form what used to be known as obscene libels, although the old common law still remains. To most people obscenity is equated with sexual acts or perversions, but it must be remembered that it also includes violence.

Obscenity is also subjective; what is considered to be obscene to one person may not be to another. The law relating to obscenity is to be found in the Obscene Publications Acts 1959 and 1964, and photographs are very often the subject of prosecution under the Act.

The Obscene Publications Act

The test of obscenity is whether the offending material would tend to deprave and corrupt those likely to be corrupted. This test can be applied to a series of photographs so that if one was deemed to be obscene, technically, the others would be similarly condemned.

In *R v Anderson* (*1972*) it was held that if a magazine consisted, as it normally does, of a number of separate articles, each had to be considered separately but, if one was deemed to be obscene, the whole publication would be contaminated by that obscenity.

Because most cases of obscenity are considered in the light of social and moral conditions obtaining at the time, the boundaries of obscenity vary enormously. It is conceivable that a jury drawn from those living in quiet and comparatively isolated country districts might well take a different view on obscenity to that of twelve men and women from a sophisticated inner city area.

It is no defence for an accused to claim that offending material could not corrupt its reading or viewing public because it was intended for those who were already corrupt.

The crux of offences under the Acts is publication of offending material. Publishing means, as far as the Obscene Publications Acts are concerned, distributing, lending, circulating, selling, giving, hiring, or offering for sale or hire.

No offence is committed by the person who buys or reads or views obscene material, and as can be seen from the previous paragraph, giving or lending of obscene material is enough to constitute publication, although nearly all prosecutions involve material which is offered for sale.

Prosecutions under the Acts normally take one of two forms. The first is seizure of the offending material after either the police or the Director of Public Prosecutions has been granted a warrant by a magistrate. The publisher has to prove to magistrates that the material is not obscene and should not be forfeited and, eventually, destroyed. There is no right of trial by jury if this course of action is brought, and in most cases forfeiture orders are made by magistrates.

Section 2(5) of the Act provides a defence if the accused can prove he had not examined the article in question and had no reason to know it was obscene. This defence is one that could not be successfully established by a photographer who took the photographs alleged to be obscene.

There is a defence of what can best be described as publication for the public good. To establish this, the defence can bring witnesses to state that in their opinion publication is justified on the grounds that it is in the interest of art, literature, science or learning. This defence was first used in 1960 when *Penguin Books* was prosecuted for publishing *Lady Chatterley's Lover*.

Since then it has been used on several occasions, and has resulted in the delightful if unedifying spectacle of expert witnesses from various fields called by the prosecution being contradicted by those called for the defence.

Summary conviction under the Act carries a fine or up to six months' imprisonment; if tried on indictment at a Crown Court an unlimited fine can be imposed, either with or without up to three years' imprisonment.

The Protection of Children Act

Closely allied to obscenity is the regrettable use of children in pornographic photographs. Until quite recently there was a gap in the law; although a photograph involving a child or children was obscene, there was no indecency on the part of the photographer as far as the child, or children, was concerned.

To fill this gap the Protection of Children Act was passed in 1978, which made it an offence to take any indecent photograph of a child. It was also made a criminal offence to distribute or show such photographs, or even possess them with the object of distributing them or showing them to others.

The Act provides a defence of having a legitimate reason for exhibiting, possessing or distributing such photographs if the accused can show he had not seen them himself or did not know, or expect them to be, indecent. This would be an almost impossible defence for the photographer who took the photographs to raise.

The offence can also be committed by a body managed by its members— a club—and penalties on conviction are the same as those quoted earlier in respect of the Obscene Publications Act.

Although the Act prohibits the taking of indecent photographs of a child, there is no definition of what constitutes indecency. In any prosecution under the Act magistrates or jurors would be expected to take an objective view although, it is submitted, because of the natural revulsion such photographs would raise in any right thinking person, it would be impossible for subjective views not to impinge on what should be a clinically judicial decision.

In any event, prosecutions can only be brought with the consent of the Director of Public Prosecutions, by the Crown Prosecution Service, and it is most likely that in arriving at his decision the Director would ask himself: would magistrates or a jury, if properly directed by a judge, be likely to find the photographs to be indecent?

The Director would in all probability ask himself a further question: is there a 51 per cent chance or more of the case resulting in a conviction?

There have not been a great many cases brought under the Act and it is likely, by the nature of pornographic pictures, that most, if not all, of these cases referred to possession of pictures rather than the actual taking of them.

Sending material through the post

Allied with obscenity as far as photographs are concerned, is the question of sending indecent or obscene material through the post, which is an offence under Section 11 of the Post Office Act 1953. This is subject to a fine of up to £1,000, if the case is dealt with in a magistrates court, or up to 12 months' imprisonment and a fine if tried at a Crown Court.

What is of particular interest in a prosecution under the Post Office Act is that the test of what is obscene is different to that laid down in the Obscene Publications Act. The section specifically refers to matter which is "grossly offensive or of an indecent or obscene character".

To obtain convictions under the Obscene Publication Acts it is necessary to show that the material has a tendency to corrupt or deprave, which is a much higher standard than "grossly offensive or of an indecent or obscene character".

This point was underlined in *R v Anderson* in 1974, which referred to a publication called *Oz* which was convicted of offences under the Obscene Publications Act and the Post Office Act. On appeal the conviction of the editor under the Obscene Publications Act was quashed, but those under the Post Office Act upheld.

The problem of sending photographs through the post which may fall foul of the Post Office Act is one which faces commercial firms of developers and printers. Most of the major firms, if they are in doubt about photographs and negatives, usually ask the person who submitted them for processing to collect them, so there is no possibility of the firm committing an offence.

Although lack of definition of what is obscene, indecent or grossly offensive may seem tiresome, it must be remembered that it is humanly impossible to create a definition. Furthermore, the advantage of what some might think to be too widely drawn an offence, is that it enables the social morals of the time to be taken into account before a prosecution is launched.

Other offences

There are a number of other offences concerning obscenity many of which are rarely used. One is the Vagrancy Acts 1824 and 1898, which creates the offence of exposing to view in a public place an obscene or indecent picture, with a penalty of a fine and/or three months' imprisonment.

It must also be remembered that obscene or indecent photographs may be subject to local bye-laws, although prosecutions under them are likely to be rare as a photograph which is obscene or indecent, is far more likely to be the subject of a prosecution under one or other of the Acts discussed in this chapter.

CHAPTER FIVE

Prohibitions and
Restrictions—Official Secrets

One of the oddities of law in this country is that, not having a written constitution, there is no legislation which clearly states what a citizen can do. The rights of a citizen are often outlined and contained in legislation, as will be seen in later chapters in this book which deal with consumer protection.

But there is very little in the law which states what a citizen can do: rather, our law—especially the criminal law—states what can *not* be done. As far as this chapter in particular is concerned, it will concentrate on when it is against the law to take photographs. In this respect it is worth remembering that we are dealing with the criminal law, which contains provisions for fines and/or imprisonment as the ultimate sanction a court can impose to mark society's displeasure for those who break the law either innocently or wilfully.

One of the main elements of criminal law, indeed the touchstone which runs through most legislation which contains penal sanctions, is contained in the Latin expression *actus non facit reum nisi mens sit rea*, which means that an act does not of itself constitute guilt unless there is a guilty mind or intention. Quite simply this can be explained as the intention to commit a criminal offence; thus, a person can, to give a simple example, take a sum of money from a shop till, but commits no offence unless the removal of the money is accompanied by an intention not to return it, thus depriving the owner permanently of his money.

There is also what is known to the law as an absolute offence, in which it is not necessary to prove a guilty mind or an intention to commit the offence; the mere commission of the offence is sufficient to convict the person concerned. This type of offence is most usually found in road traffic cases, or in legislation passed to enforce standards of public conduct.

There are a number of words used in legislation which the courts have over the years construed as meaning that *mens rea*—guilty mind or intention—is required before a person can be found guilty. "Knowingly", "wilfully", "maliciously", "permitting" or "suffering" when used in legislation which has a penal element, are construed by courts as denoting the necessity of proving an accused person had a guilty mind or intention before he or she can be convicted of an offence where this element is required.

With this explanation, it is now possible to look at those criminal offences a photographer can be vulnerable to during the course of his employment or following his hobby.

The Official Secrets Act

A photographer is particularly at risk when taking photographs of military equipment or installations, as he may be in breach of the Official Secrets Acts of 1911, 1920 and 1939, which the courts construe as one Act.

Unfortunately the Acts have been drafted, either intentionally or by accident, in such a way that a person who has no intention of passing information of a confidential or secret nature can be ensnared, and photographers are particularly at risk.

It is necessary to look at the Acts in detail. Section 1 of the 1911 Act makes it an offence punishable by up to 14 years imprisonment if a person for any purpose prejudicial to the safety or interest of the state—

(1) Approaches, inspects, passes over or is in the neighbourhood of or enters any prohibited place;

(2) Makes any sketch, plan, model or note which might be or is intended to be, useful to an enemy; and,

(3) Obtains, collects, records or communicates to any person information that might be, or is intended to be, useful to an enemy.

As can be seen this is very wide ranging and would include photographs. What then is a prohibited place within the meaning of the Act?

The answer is to be found in Section 3 of the 1911 Act as amended by the 1920 Act, and because of the importance to all photographers of its content it is set out in full, as follows:

"(a) any work of defence, arsenal, naval or air force establishment or station, factory, dockyard, mine, minefield, camp, ship, or aircraft belonging to or occupied by or on behalf of Her Majesty, or any telegraph, telephone, wireless or signal station, or office so belonging or occupied, and any place occupied by and on behalf of Her Majesty and used for the purpose of building, repairing, making or storing any munitions of war, or any sketches, note or model relating thereto, or for the purpose of getting any metals, oil or mineral of use in time of war;

(b) any place not belonging to Her Majesty where any munitions of war, or any sketches, etc., relating thereto, are made, repaired gotten or stored under contract with, or with any person on behalf of, Her Majesty;

(c) any place belonging to or used for the purposes of Her Majesty which is for the time being declared by order of a Secretary of State to be a prohibited place for the purposes of this section on the ground that information with respect thereto, or damage thereto, would be useful to an enemy: and,

(d) any railway, road, way or channel, or other means of communication by land or water (including any works of structure for gas, water, electricity works or other works of a public character, or any place where munitions of war, or any sketches, etc. . . . relating thereto are being made, repaired, or stored otherwise than on behalf of Her Majesty, which is for the time being declared by order of a Secretary of State to be a prohibited place for the purposes of this section, on the ground that information with respect thereto, or the destruction or obstruction thereof, would be useful to an enemy."

Interpretation of the Act

The above section repays careful study, for in effect it is capable of ensnaring any photographer who innocently takes a photograph of any of these many and varied places. However, prosecutions under the Official Secrets Acts can only be brought with the consent of the Attorney-General and it is, perhaps, fortunate that usually a robust and commonsense view is taken. In past years photographs have appeared of the top secret Government Communications Headquarters in Cheltenham which, strictly speaking, is an offence. Obviously, the fact that the particular building is well known to be what in fact it is, means that photographing the exterior is likely to do little harm to state security.

Most buildings which are covered by the Official Secrets Acts display a notice to this effect, but photographers are most at risk if they take photographs of dramatic pieces of military equipment such as aeroplanes, tanks, guns, vessels, etc. These carry no notices saying they are prohibited places, but in many cases they are covered by the Acts and may even be the subject of a D Notice.

Throughout Section 1 of the Act runs the thread that receiving information must be for a purpose prejudicial to the interests of the State, but nowhere is there a definition of what is meant by the term "prejudicial"; indeed, it seems that "prejudicial" can by anything an Attorney-General of the day considers so to be.

This was exemplified in 1962 when six members of what was then known as the Committee of 100, which was strongly opposed to nuclear weapons, staged a sit down at an East Anglian airfield and were arrested and charged under Section 1 of the Act. There was no question of espionage involved, but the Attorney-General of the day felt that the sit down, peaceful though it was, amounted to sabotage.

The six were convicted and appealed. The appeal was finally heard by the House of Lords who upheld the conviction.

So it presents little difficulty for an Attorney-General of the day to order a prosecution against a photographer, who might in no way be connected with any foreign espionage system but who does enter a prohibited place unlawfully.

Section 2 and the Official Secrets Bill

Perhaps the most criticised of all penal legislation has been Section 2 of the Official Secrets Acts. Known as the "catch-all" section, its scope has been criticised and rightly so, by members of the judiciary, lawyers, journalists and civil libertarians, to say nothing of members of both Houses of Parliament.

It was known as the "catch-all" section because it made it an offence for a person to reveal and/or publish a wide range of information which had no bearing whatsoever on the security of the realm. Readers of the first edition of this book will be familiar with the wide ranging samples quoted.

Now the Government has introduced the Official Secrets Bill, which is described as a "liberalising measure". Suffice it to say that this bill has encountered strong opposition from both sides of the House of Commons as well as from journalists and those interested in civil liberties.

Under the proposed new legislation a category of "protected information" will be created which falls under six heads. In five of these categories it is a defence to prove that no harm was done, and the prosecution has to prove harm. The five categories are:

Defence;
Security and intelligence;
International relations;
Confidential Government to Government information; and
Information that impedes detection of crime or the apprehension and prosecution of offenders, etc.

The sixth category refers to the publication of information about the interception of mail, the tapping of telephones, etc., and here it will be assumed that harm *will* be done.

It will be no defence to claim that the information has already been published, or that it was in the public interest to be published or that the damage created by its publication was less than would have been the case if the information had not been published.

The arguments which have ranged inside and outside of Parliament over the Bill need not be rehearsed in this book and, indeed, it is arguable that photographers are, in the main, unlikely to fall foul of the proposed new secrets legislation unless they work for the news media.

Protection of sources

There is one other section of the 1920 Act which can be applied in a particularly restrictive and some would say oppressive manner, to photographers, especially those in the media who may have been supplied with photographs or negatives which are the subject of prohibition under the Act. Section 6 reads:

"(1) Where a chief officer of police is satisfied that there is reasonable ground for suspecting that an offence under Section 1 (of the 1911 Act) has been committed and for believing that any person is able to furnish information as to the offence, he may apply to the Secretary of State for permission to exercise the powers conferred by the Secretary of State and, if such permission is granted, he may authorise a superintendent of police, or any police officer not below the rank of inspector, to require the person believed to be able to furnish information to give any information in his power relating to the offence or suspected offence . . ."

The section also states that failing to comply with the requirement, or giving false information, can be punished with up to two years' imprisonment if tried on indictment, or if tried at a magistrates court three months' imprisonment or a fine.

It can be seen that this section faces a professional journalist or news photographer with a moral dilemma: does he follow the unwritten journalistic code of protecting his sources and face the threat of prosecution, or does he violate the code and reveal sources?

Further, in the case of an emergency a chief officer may invoke Section 6 without obtaining the Home Secretary's permission, provided he informs the Minister at a later date. Search warrants, which normally have to be issued by a magistrate, are not needed under the Act in a case of emergency, and enable the police to enter premises and search and seize anything which is reasonably relevant to an offence under the Act.

D Notices

Closely allied to the question of Official Secrets is the D Notice system, as the Defence, Press and Broadcasting Committee's notices are known to the media. This committee is composed of Government, press, and broadcasting representatives and is effectively a self-censorship system.

The notices are issued after discussion by the committee, identify those areas considered to be dangerous and/or sensitive to State security, and offer guidance on how matters subject to a D Notice may be discussed, if at all.

D Notices do not have any force in law, but it would be a brave, if albeit foolhardy, editor who ignored one, as behind the notice stands the widespread powers of the Official Secrets Act.

CHAPTER SIX

Prohibitions and Restrictions—The Courts

The most well known court building in the country is the Old Bailey, or the Central Criminal Court to give its correct name, in the City of London. It has been photographed countless times, and will doubtless continue to be an object of great interest to photographers.

It is, however, an offence against Section 41 of the Criminal Justice Act 1925 to take any photograph, or make any portrait or sketch in court, and this also applies to persons entering or leaving the court or its precincts.

Photography in the courts

Unfortunately the photographer will find there is no definition of what the precincts of the court are: they can, in fact, be anything the court decides.

Newspaper photographers who cover the courts are fully aware of the rules against photographing inside the court or the precincts, and take every effort to ensure that, when taking photographs of anyone involved in a case either entering or leaving a court, the court itself is not shown.

It is the enthusiastic amateur or the foreign newspaper photographer who is most likely to fall foul of the law in this respect. In many of the major cities of England and Wales, courts are held in historic buildings which are worthy of a photograph in their own right.

Nothing could make a better picture than to photograph a High Court judge in his red robes and with his retinue, entering or leaving the court. But to take such a photograph is inviting trouble, as an amateur photographer discovered some years ago in Nottingham. He was promptly arrested, brought in front of the judge, and fined.

On the other hand, during the A6 murder trial at Bedford in 1961, a *cause celebre* whose echoes are occasionally heard even today, the late Mr Justice Gorman fully appreciated the reality of the situation and agreed with newspaper photographers to permit them, on one occasion only, to take a photograph of him leaving the court to go to his lodgings.

This was a sensible approach which was respected and observed by cameramen attending the trial. Today it is not uncommon for a judge to leave a court to take evidence from a witness in hospital, or to visit a location which plays an important role in a trial.

Professional cameramen working for newspapers know that an approach to the judge's clerk for guidance as far as photographs are concerned, will often result in a positive reply, even though there may be qualifications.

It is the photographer who is unaware of the law who is most likely to get into trouble, especially those who work for a foreign publication. During the trial of Peter Sutcliffe, the "Yorkshire Ripper", at the Old Bailey, a photographer for a German magazine took a photograph inside the court using sophisticated equipment so that his actions went unnoticed.

The photograph was published, and when publication was brought to the attention of the judge, the London editor of the magazine, who had no knowledge of the taking of the photograph, was banned from attending the rest of the trial.

Contempt of court

The greatest risk of legal action following the publication of photographs comes from contempt of court, when publication is likely to create a substantial risk that the course of justice in particular court proceedings will be seriously impaired.

To understand the rationale behind what is commonly known as publications being in contempt of court, a look at the historical background is of help.

Until quite recently contempt was a common law offence, that is an offence created not by Act of Parliament but by custom, usage and decisions of courts going back many centuries.

As far as publishing contempt is concerned, it consists, mainly, of actions likely to impair the course of justice, and photographs have often resulted in newspapers being prosecuted for such offences.

The issue of identity

In most cases publication of a photograph will only constitute contempt if identity is likely to be an issue in a forthcoming trial. In 1927 the *Daily Mirror* was held to be in contempt for publishing a photograph of an accused person on the morning of the day he was due to appear on an identity parade, and Lord Hewart, the then Lord Chief Justice, observed there was a duty to refrain from publication where it was apparent to a reasonable man that a question of identity (in a trial) arises. Much later when then Young Liberal activist Peter Hain was arrested and charged with robbing a bank, the *Evening Standard* published a photograph of him under the heading: "I'm no bank robber". This was also held to be contempt, as a question of identity arose. In the event Peter Hain was rightly acquitted.

Contempt in Scotland

It is in Scotland that there have been several decisions in the not too distant past concerning contempt of court by publication of photographs. Scotland has a different legal system to that which obtains in England and Wales. Scottish law embodies legal principles drawn from Roman law, and common law which derives from the law which obtains in England and Wales.

For the purpose of this chapter it is only necessary to look at Scottish decisions regarding contempt, decisions which have been accepted generally as being much tougher than those of English law, and were judge made.

In 1960 the *Scottish Daily Mail* was fined £5,000 and its editor £500 for publishing an article and picture about a double murderer, and as a result of the judgement of Lord Clyde in that case, Scottish newspapers felt themselves to be very much restricted as far as what they could write once the police were investigating a crime.

In the same year the Glasgow based newspaper the *Daily Record* was fined

£7,500 and the editor £500 for publishing the photograph of a footballer who had been arrested on indecency charges.

A photograph figured in a case in 1978. London Weekend Television and three executives were fined a total of £61,000 for contempt, for screening a photograph of a nursing sister and referring to her trial the following day in Edinburgh Sheriff Court.

The interesting point is that the indictment against the nurse was dropped. In the hearing of the case against LWT and its three executives, Lord Emslie, Scotland's Lord Justice General, said there was no difficulty in accepting that there was no hard and fast rule that publication of an accused person's photograph would always be contempt.

Lord Emslie added, however, that a photograph of an accused would only constitute contempt where a question of identity had or might arise, and where the publication of the photograph was calculated to prejudice the prospect of a fair trial.

Although such a ruling would be persuasive rather than binding on an English court, it confirmed what had been the basis of what may be termed photographic contempt in England and Wales; that there is no contempt in publishing the photograph of an accused person unless identity is in dispute.

The Contempt of Court Act 1981

It must not be thought that prejudice applies only to the defence in a criminal court. It can apply equally well to publication of anything which might affect the case for the prosecution.

There is a second reason for the contempt rule as far as publishing photographs of accused persons before their trial is concerned. The fact that a photograph has been published could well influence a witness to positively identify the accused when, without that photograph, identification may not have taken place in court or, if it did, may be uncertain and qualified.

Greater certainty now exists since the Contempt of Court Act 1981, which was claimed by the Government to reform and liberalise common law contempt. However, despite the Act, common law contempt can still be committed.

Under the Act any writing, speech or broadcast can be treated as contempt regardless of intent, if it creates a substantial risk that the course of justice in the proceedings in question—and these proceedings can be civil as well as criminal—will be seriously prejudiced.

Proceedings are deemed to be active as far as criminal proceedings are concerned if a person has been arrested, or a warrant for arrest or summons to appear in court has been issued.

In theory this is fine; in practice, it creates great difficulty, for an editor may have no way of knowing if an arrest has been made or a warrant or summons issued, although there is a defence that if, at the time of publication, and having taken all reasonable care the editor, writer or publisher, did not know and had no reason to suspect, that proceedings were active.

The same defence applies to contempt of civil proceedings, which are said to be active when the case is set down for trial or a date fixed for the action to be heard. Again this poses difficulties in knowing when this stage in litigation has been reached.

As far as photographs are concerned, it is generally assumed that there will be no contempt in England and Wales in publishing a photograph provided identification is not in issue, but it may not be until the trial of a case that it is finally established that identity is not an issue.

Photographs of a crime

From time to time a photographer is able to take photographs of a crime actually being committed. Very often this is in the case of crowd violence during a demonstration or at a football match.

Would publication of such photographs constitute contempt of court? It is submitted that the answer must be no. Provided the photographs have not been tampered with, they are in fact evidence of the crime being committed. In the event of a trial the photographs would in all probability be placed before magistrates or a jury as "best evidence", with the photographer being called to prove he took the pictures and that they had not been tampered with.

If the photograph could be capable of bearing two interpretations, it is for the defence to demonstrate this fact to the tribunal. Publication of such photographs would only be likely to be contempt if accompanied by an article or caption making a positive assertion that those pictured were guilty of the offence depicted in the photograph.

Police access to photographs

However, since this book was first published the Police and Criminal Evidence Act 1984 has come into effect, which gives the police new powers of access to material which would be of substantial value in investigating a serious arrestable offence and would be likely to be relevant evidence.

An arrestable offence is one where the penalty on first conviction can be of at least five years imprisonment or, in the case of murder, where the penalty is fixed by statute. Taking a car without authority or driving with excess of alcohol in the blood are also arrestable offences even though the penalties are less than five years imprisonment.

Furthermore, a police officer may arrest without a warrant if he suspects a person of having committed an arrestable offence.

Under the Act the police can apply to a circuit judge for an order for them to have access to journalistic material, but the particular target of the request has to be given an opportunity to resist the application in court.

There are, however, two safeguards available to the media, excluded material and special procedure material.

In the case of excluded material the police can obtain an order only if they had power under the old law to obtain a search warrant—if the material had been stolen—or an offence under the Official Secrets Act was suspected. Excluded material includes journalistic material held in confidence and consisting of documents or records.

Special procedure material includes material not held in confidence, such as photographs, and a judge can make an order giving the police access to such material if he rules it is in the public interest so to do.

So what is journalistic material? Under the Act it is defined as material "acquired or created for the purpose of journalism".

As far as special procedure material is concerned most, if not all, of what cases there have been under the Act refer to photographs.

Following riots in the St. Paul's area of Bristol, the police in 1986 sought untransmitted television newsreel footage from two television companies, and unpublished news photographs taken by a freelance picture agency and photographers of the *Bristol Evening Post* and *Western Daily Press*.

Having been refused, the police applied to a judge at Bristol Crown Court for an order under the Act. This was granted, although the judge did not ask the police to specify offences which had been committed nor the relevance or probative value of the material required. The police asked for 190 pictures and television footage taken between specific times.

It was argued in vain that to grant the police request would not be in the public interest as it would compromise the impartiality of the media and endanger photographers at future incidents if those participating knew such an order could be made. Nevertheless, the judge ruled that the public interest in catching criminals outweighed these arguments.

Although the case applied to the media it is not beyond the realms of possibility that an amateur photographer who took similar photographs could be forced to hand over prints and negatives to the police.

As far as the media is concerned police need not ask for an order to produce material, including photographs, for under the Act the police can apply to a judge for a search warrant, and if this step is taken the paper does not have to be informed or have the right to be heard.

If this step is taken, and again it can apply to an independent photographer, the judge must be satisfied that not only the criteria already referred to exists—the arrestable offence, etc.—but that one of the following circumstances apply:

It is not practicable to communicate with anyone entitled to grant entry to the premises;
It is not practicable to communicate with anyone entitled to grant access to the material;
That the material contains information which is subject to an obligation of secrecy or a restriction on disclosure by statute—as would be material subject to the Official Secrets Act under the proposed Official Secrets Bill when enacted—and is likely to be disclosed in breach of that obligation if a search warrant is not issued;
That serving a notice of an order to produce might seriously prejudice an investigation of a crime.

Reporting restrictions

There are, of course, no restrictions on naming defendants or witnesses in cases in Magistrates Courts or Crown Courts, although there are exceptions to this as far as photographs are concerned. But in cases which are committed for trial from magistrates courts—unless reporting restrictions are lifted—details of a report are limited to the following ten points:

Name of court and of the examining magistrate or justices;
Name(s), address(es) and occupations of parties and witnesses and the age of defendant(s) and witnesses;
The offence(s) with which the defendant(s) is charged or a summary of them;
Names of solicitors and counsel in the proceedings;
The decision of the court to commit for trial and the decisions on any defendant(s) not committed;
Charges on which the defendant(s) is committed or a summary of them and the court to which committed;
The date and place to which any committal is adjourned;
Any arrangements as to bail on adjournment or committal;
Whether legal aid was granted; and,
Any decision of the court to lift or not to lift reporting restrictions.

On first sight of the above list of restrictions, it may appear there is nothing which prohibits a photograph of the accused being published, and therein lies trouble for the media photographer.

Many committals for trial are done on paper; this means that if the accused is legally represented and agrees to the course of action, all the prosecution needs to do is to serve statements of evidence on the accused's legal representative and hand copies to the examining justices for the case to be sent for trial as a pure formality.

Unfortunately for the photographer, he does not know whether or not identity is going to be an issue; publication of a photograph may help to sway the mind of witnesses that the man they saw was, in fact, the man whose photograph appeared as being a defendant.

It is, of course, a different matter if the evidence is heard by magistrates—whether or not reporting restrictions are lifted—but even then there is danger, as witnesses to identity may not be cross-examined until the trial itself.

Publication of a photograph of an accused in circumstances where mistaken identity is the sole issue could, as discussed earlier, constitute contempt.

Sexual offences

Under the Sexual Offences (Amendment) Act 1976, Sections 4, 5 and 6 prohibited publication of anything which would identify the defendant, unless he is convicted, or the complainant, in any proceedings for rape, attempted rape, aiding, abetting, counselling and procuring rape. Although only a man can commit rape or attempted rape, a woman can be convicted of counselling, procuring, aiding or abetting the offence.

This legislation was amended by the Criminal Justice Act 1988 which added two more offences subject to restrictions—conspiracy to rape and burglary with intent to rape—and also lifted the shield of anonymity from the defendant who can now be named in connection with these offences and, subject to any other restrictions which might apply under the law relating to contempt or identification of juveniles, can also be identified by way of a published photograph.

On the other hand the Criminal Justice Act 1988 has tightened up the ban on publishing anything which would identify the complainant. It is now an offence to publish or broadcast, after an allegation of rape has been made, anything which would lead to the identification of a rape complainant or to publish any still or moving picture of her during her lifetime.

However the complainant can be identified if she gives her written consent to publication, unless it is proved that any person interfered unreasonably with her peace or comfort to gain that consent.

On this point commonsense dictates that a persistent photographer who constantly makes the life of a rape victim miserable to obtain her consent for a picture of her to be published, could not seek to say consent was genuinely given.

Two interesting points emerge from the new legislation. One is that the restrictions cover the rare instances where a woman who has been the victim of rape brings a civil action against her alleged rapist and that restrictions last for the lifetime of the woman.

So if, during the course of the rape, the woman is murdered and her killer charged with both rape and murder, the restrictions would not apply.

The complainant may still be named, however, under the terms of the Sexual Offences (Amendment) Act in the following circumstances:

If, before the trial starts, the accused satisfies a judge sitting in a Crown

Court that the lifting of restrictions is necessary for the purpose of inducing witnesses to come forward and that the conduct of his defence is likely to be substantially prejudiced if the restrictions are not lifted; or

The judge is satisfied that the woman's anonymity imposes a substantial and unreasonable restriction on reporting the trial and it is in the public interest to remove or relax the restrictions.

Juvenile Courts

It is also necessary to look at the situation involving juvenile courts, which have jurisdiction over young persons and children under 17 years of age. It is undoubtedly true that from time to time cases are heard in juvenile courts which are newsworthy and attract media interest. It has been the intention of the legislature for many years to protect juveniles from publicity following court appearances.

The Children and Young Persons Act 1933 established juvenile courts in England and Wales, and although Section 47 of the Act bars members of the public from attending these courts, bona fide representatives of newspapers and news agencies are permitted to attend.

Under Section 49 of the Act of 1933, reports of juvenile courts must not contain anything which would lead to a juvenile being identified. Section 39 of the Act specifically prohibits a photograph of a juvenile involved in court proceedings. It does not bar a photograph of a juvenile appearing as a defendant, complainant or witness in juvenile court proceedings from being taken; the bar is against publication, which is an offence.

Similar restrictions apply to a juvenile appealing against a decision of a juvenile court, to either the Crown Court or the Divisional Court.

Curiously, such restrictions against identifying juveniles do not apply when juveniles are tried with an adult in Magistrates Court or a Crown Court, or appear as a witness, although such courts do have the power, which is generally exercised, to order that anything which may identify a juvenile should not be published. Newspapers themselves, aware of this anomoly in the law, quite often have house rules which result in a voluntary ban on identifying juveniles.

Magistrates in juvenile courts and the Home Secretary are empowered to lift restrictions on naming a juvenile, but only to avoid injustice to that particular individual.

Wards of court, persons under the age of 18 who have had a court appointed guardian to look after them and their interests, are also protected from identification, as are children who figure in adoption proceedings.

Juvenile proceedings in Scotland

The situation in Scotland is different as far as juveniles are concerned. Since 1971 justice is dispensed at Children's Hearings following the passing of the Social Work (Scotland) Act 1968, which abolished juvenile courts and instituted a system which was orientated towards the treatment of offenders. There is a bar on the identification of children appearing at Children's Hearings, and also on persons up to the age of 18 if they are under a form of supervision imposed by one of the hearings.

But children who have committed certain crimes—murder, attempted murder, rape, assault to the danger of life, possession of offensive weapons, offences under the Road Traffic Acts which carry disqualification, and offences where the child is charged with an adult, continue to be prosecuted in the High Court or Sheriff Court. This also may be extended to a child who has committed an offence which, in the opinion of the prosecutor, merits prosecution in court in the public interest.

Nevertheless, no child appearing before a Children's Hearing, or hearings in a Sheriff Court or an appeal court, can be identified, and under the Criminal Justice (Scotland) Act 1980, children appearing in criminal proceedings as either an accused person, witnesses or victims, may not be identified. This prohibition does not apply if the person under 16 is a witness only, unless the court directs otherwise.

CHAPTER SEVEN

Prohibitions and Restrictions—Public Places

By the very nature of life, from time to time there are major disasters: air and train crashes, multiple pile-ups on a motorway, natural disasters such as floods. It is at times like these, coupled with demonstrations and what may be best described as occasions concerning the security of a particular person, when photographers are most likely to fall foul of the criminal law.

From time to time cases are reported of photographers being arrested either for obstruction or for behaviour likely to cause a breach of the peace. To the photographer concerned the action of the police is seen as arbitrary at its best and dictatorial at its worst. It is within the pages of a book of this type that the problem can be considered in a way which is devoid of emotion.

The risk of arrest

Whenever a photographer is arrested while following his profession, or even hobby, in recording on film events such as those described above, reason on both sides often seems to fly out of the window.

Subject to restrictions on photography described in previous chapters, it is not an offence to take photographs of disasters or major incidents, but discretion should be observed at all times.

At the time of a major disaster there is no doubt that the police have an onerous and thankless task to perform. Not only are they part of the essential services involved in rescue operations, they are also responsible for ensuring that such operations are carried out with the minimum of interference to other rescue services. It is regrettable that on many occasions photographers are seen as obstacles to be removed from the scene.

Consequently photographers are unwittingly and unfairly cast in the role of a minor villain, and the police show little sympathy with cameramen who exercise their rights to take pictures.

If arrests follow—and this applies not only to disasters but also to demonstrations—the charge preferred is invariably using behaviour which, in London, is charged under the Metropolitan Police Act 1839, and in the rest of England and Wales under the Public Order Act 1936.

Under the former Act, it is an offence for any person to use threatening, abusive or insulting words or behaviour with intent to provoke a breach of the peace or whereby a breach of the peace may be occasioned.

Under the Public Order Act S.5 as amended by the Race Relations Act 1965 and the Criminal Law Act 1977 Schedule 1, the wording is as follows:

"Any person who in any public place or at any public meeting uses threatening abusive or insulting words or behaviour with intent to provoke a breach of the peace or whereby a breach of the peace is likely to be occasioned, shall be guilty of an offence . . . "

Demonstrations and marches

It is under this Act that photographers are most at risk when covering demonstrations or marches, and this will be dealt with first. There is no doubt that members of many extremist organisations at both ends of the political spectrum dislike being photographed taking part in marches or demonstrations.

Consequently, a photographer, by pointing a camera at such people, can either cause a breach of the peace or be likely to, but such an action must be more than one calculated to cause annoyance.

What is unfortunate in these circumstances is that many policemen, anxious to preserve the peace, take a subjective rather than an objective view of taking photographs and assume, sometimes incorrectly, that a breach of the peace is most likely. The photographer is therefore arrested, and has the unenviable task of persuading a magistrate or magistrates that his action did not, or was unlikely to, cause a breach of the peace. Under this Act penalty on conviction is imprisonment for no more than six months and/or a fine.

It must be stressed that this offence is most likely to be charged under the Public Order Act, which is far more draconian in terms of punishment than conviction under the Metropolitan Police Act.

Disasters and other major incidents

It is under the Metropolitan Police Act or similar legislation for the rest of the country, that a photographer is likely to be charged at scenes of a disaster or major incident.

Only a few years ago a cameraman was arrested and convicted under just such a provision, for persisting in taking a photograph of an Army officer defusing a bomb placed by the IRA. The reasoning behind this particular arrest was that the officer had protested at having his photograph taken because of probable reprisals against himself or his family if he was identified.

There is no doubt that photographers unintentionally could get in the way of rescue workers at the time of a disaster when emotions are high, and this could lead to an exchange of heated words or blows.

Not unnaturally, the police would try to obviate such an occurrence and leave rescue workers to get on with their jobs unimpeded, by arresting the photographer concerned and charging him with insulting behaviour.

It must be remembered that it is not necessary for a breach of the peace to take place; it is only necessary for a likelihood of such an event happening for a charge to be successfully laid.

Obstruction

Another arm which police can and do use with success is to arrest photographers who do not move when ordered to do so, and this can lead to other charges in which the word obstruction figures prominently.

Section 121 of the Highways Act 1959 provides that if a person without lawful authority or excuse in any way wilfully obstructs the free passage along a highway he is guilty of an offence.

The word wilfully has a multitude of meanings, but can generally be assumed to mean exercise of free will, which would surely be the case as far as a photographer is concerned.

The other offence in which the word obstruction is used in the charge is a more serious one, and is likely to be brought against a photographer who persists in taking photographs and argues with a police constable. "Any person who resists or wilfully obstructs a constable in the execution of his duty . . . shall be guilty of an offence and liable on summary conviction to not more than a months' imprisonment or a fine or both" under Section 51 of the Police Act 1964.

A photographer charged with this offence may find it more difficult to mount a defence, as the meaning of wilfully in this instance was decided in 1977 to mean an intention to obstruct the constable *in the sense of making it more difficult for him*. It is not difficult to see how a harrassed policeman at the scene of a disaster or incident may well think a photographer refusing to move or arguing is making it more difficult for the policemen to carry out his duties.

Disasters and incidents of the type discussed do not always occur on or in public land; they frequently happen on private land, and here the photographer is on safer ground. Provided he has permission to be on the land a photographer, although still liable to arrest for obstruction or insulting behaviour, cannot legally be asked to move on. He has permission to be on the land, and his rights in this respect are discussed in chapter 9.

Railways

Railways are a difficult proposition: it is an offence under a number of statutes appertaining to railways, going back to the Railway Regulation Act 1840, to wilfully obstruct or impede any agent or officer of the railway in the execution of his duty, and also to wilfully trespass on the railway itself, stations, works or premises. It is worth noting in this respect that it is not only when photographing railway accidents that a photographer is at risk. There are other occasions when a photographer may find himself technically trespassing for the sake of a dramatic photograph. The penalty for committing the offence is a fine or a term of imprisonment not exceeding one month. Similar provisions apply to London Transport's underground railway and licensed aerodromes, while certain docks are covered by bye-laws.

Rights and remedies

The above is a formidable list of traps for photographers, but there are counter balances to be found, mostly in the civil law, which are based on old established rights created over the centuries to protect the person and property of the individual.

For the purpose of this part of the chapter, it is assumed the photographer is not trespassing, nor is he obstructing a constable in the execution of his duty or using behaviour which could occasion a breach of the peace.

Perhaps the most drastic civil remedy which could be brought against a constable, or any other person who unlawfully restrains a citizen of this country, or even a foreign visitor, is the tort of false imprisonment.

A tort is a civil wrong, and the law broadly recognises that for every wrong there is a legal remedy. *Injuria* is a legal concept which means an injury having legal consequences, and this is distinguished from *damnum* which is the damage suffered. The two do not always go together, as it is possible for a person to suffer damage without having a legal remedy; to claim for harm done there must be a violation of a legal right, and even an act done with malice to another does not give rise to a cause of action unless a legal right is violated.

False imprisonment

False imprisonment is the unauthorised bodily restraint of a person without lawful authority. Such a situation could arise, as far as a photographer is concerned, when either a constable, official or even ordinary citizen, restrains the photographer's movements.

It is not necessary for a person to be imprisoned in the popular sense of being locked up. The essence of this tort is that the restriction of a person's freedom of movement is absolute. Thus a photographer who is restricted unlawfully from continuing in a forward direction towards, say, the scene of an incident, would not have a case if he is free to move in another direction, even if it is not the way he wishes to go.

On the other hand, if a photographer was to find himself in an alleyway with a dead end between high buildings and his only way out barred, he would have a strong case of false imprisonment, as his freedom of movement is absolutely restrained in the sense that he cannot leave the blind alleyway.

Cases of false imprisonment are a rarity, although it is possible to think of situations analogous to the one discussed which photographers may have faced in the past, or are likely to encounter in the future.

Assault

It is most likely that a photographer would seek to enforce his rights by way of compensation for injury he has suffered wrongly, in an action for assault and/or battery, but it must be remembered that there has to be a legal cause of action. Being jostled in a crowd is insufficient, as the law presumes that, by joining a crowd, a person consents to any jostling which may follow.

It is necessary to understand the difference in law between assault and battery. Assault, contrary to what most people think, is not striking a blow which actually lands on a person. It is an attempt or threat or apply such force which constitutes the tort of assault. The situation must be such that the person offering violence is in a position to carry out the threat, and puts the person to whom it is offered in fear of such violence.

At one time it was considered that the mere uttering of a threat would not constitute assault, but in *Ansell v Thomas (1974)* the Court of Appeal held that a threat to use force was sufficient to found an action for assault.

Battery is the intention to bring any material object onto the person of another, provided there is sufficient use of force to give rise to battery. It is interesting to note that some academic lawyers have put forward the proposition that the unauthorised taking of a photograph with a flash might be battery because the projection of throwing the sharp light from a flash, causing personal discomfort, would constitute this tort.

Before photographers consider bringing an action for assault and/or battery, they or their legal advisers will no doubt consider the defences available to the person to be sued. One of the most important is that of self-defence.

This defence extends to the protection of those a person has the moral or legal obligation to protect. It is possible that a person seeking to avoid publicity for himself or his family would resort to assault and/or battery to avoid any publicity that publication of a photograph might bring. Indeed, it need not be to avoid unwelcome publicity; the situation could arise from a street photographer whose persistence is causing embarrassment, or a person taking candid camera shots. Whether in these circumstances self-defence would be a valid defence to a civil action would depend on the circumstances of the individual case.

What must be remembered is that a photographer, or any other person, who wishes to be recompensed for any hurt suffered, should not bring an action for assault in the magistrate's court. Under SS *44–45* of the Offences Against the Persons Act 1861, if a summary prosecution is launched and the accused convicted and punished, even if such a punishment is no more than an absolute discharge, no further action or civil proceedings may be taken in respect of that particular incident. Similarly, if the case is dismissed and magistrates issue a certificate of dismissal, any further action is barred.

Furthermore trespass to the person by way of assault and/or battery is not actionable in itself.

To successfully sustain a prosecution, the plaintiff has to prove either negligence or intention on the part of the defendant, and this is a matter of fact rather than of law. Damages which may be awarded will vary from case to case, and the greater the injury suffered the higher the damages are likely to be.

If a case of false imprisonment is successful, aggravated damages may be awarded for any humiliation the plaintiff has suffered as well as normal damages.

Interference with cameras or film

It is not uncommon for photographers to have their cameras seized and damaged, or handed back to them with the film ripped out. When this happens another tort arises, that of trespass to property; in most cases however any civil action is most likely to be accompanied by the tort of trespass to the person, for the very act of seizing the camera is likely to be accompanied by an assault.

The Torts (Interference with Goods) Act 1977 defines wrongful interference as including trespass to goods, conversion of goods, negligence or any other act which results in damage to goods or to a person's interest in goods.

For the purpose of discussing wrongful interference with goods by trespass, it will be assumed that the photographer is either the owner of the camera, or has a legal right to have it in his possession, for the right of possession has to exist at the time the wrongful interference is committed. The plaintiff must also prove a direct interference with the goods.

This would not be difficult in the case where a camera is seized or merely pushed aside, for the interference is self-evident.

The problem a photographer faces in bringing an action for trespass to goods is quantum of damages to be recovered. If a camera is damaged, or a film ripped out, the question of quantum is not difficult: it is the value of the repair or the film.

Where the problem really begins is how to quantify the value of the pictures already taken on the destroyed film, or those which would have been taken if the camera was not damaged. If the incident was a newsworthy one, for which a freelance or even an amateur photographer could expect to be paid for the pictures, this must be taken into account.

In such a case, the photographer must be able to demonstrate to a court that had he not been stopped by damage to camera or to film, his photographs would have been worth a particular sum of money to him by virtue of their news value.

To prove this, it would be necessary for the photographer to produce evidence of what a particular publication would have paid for dramatic photographs. There would be no difficulty, however, if the photographer had been commissioned to take photographs for a quoted fee.

An intriguing point arises when consideration is given to the case of the commissioned freelance referred to in the previous paragraph, or the photographer employed by a newspaper or magazine assigned to photo-graph a newsworthy incident. In both instances the photographer loses nothing: the commissioned freelance may well receive his fee in all the circumstances, while the staff photographer has suffered no monetary loss by not getting photographs.

If, as a result of damage to the camera and/or film, the newspaper or magazine has suffered loss of circulation or the possibility of selling photo-graphs to overseas or non-competing publications, they must have a cause for action as the photographer is acting on their behalf. But here again, it is necessary for loss to be quantified, and on such an ephemeral and intangible field as newsworthiness, this is difficult to establish—although not impossible.

Who to sue?

The next question which arises is: who to sue? If the person who has committed trespass to either the person of the photographer and/or trespass to goods by way of damage to camera and film is an individual, he or she is the person on whom a County Court summons or High Court writ should be served.

If the person is the servant (the legal term for an employee) or the agent of an individual or a company, both individual and the company or employer should be sued, as the former can be said to be acting on behalf of the latter.

Before 1947 the Crown enjoyed immunity from being sued for either tort or breach of contract, on the grounds of the old legal maxim that the King (or Queen) can do no harm. But in that year the Crown Proceedings Act was passed, with the result that the Crown—that is the Government—is now liable in the same way as any subject. But neither the Crown or the authority which appoints and pays the police are liable for torts committed by the police.

However, S 48(1) of the Police Act 1964 makes the chief officer of police for any police area liable for the torts committed by police officers, and the Act also provides for any damages and costs awarded against the chief officer of police to be paid out of police funds.

Another question to be answered is what court to sue in. If damages claimed are what are known as liquidated—that is where the amount sought is known—or if they are unliquidated but the total is not more than £5,000, the proper forum for the action is the local county court. Above £5,000, or unless there is a particularly difficult point of law to be resolved, the forum is the High Court.

CHAPTER 8

A Few Further Restrictions

There are a few other areas where certain prohibitions and restrictions apply, and these will be dealt with in this chapter.

Employment of children

Under the Children's and Young Persons Act 1933 and 1963 it is an offence to employ children under the age of 13. Until 1983 it had been thought that those who used child models for advertising purposes in still photography were covered by the Children (Performances) Regulations 1968.

This Act covers children appearing in "any performance recorded (by whatever means) with a view to its use in a broadcast or in a film intended for public exhibition". Some model agencies had thought this covered children appearing in still photographs for advertising purposes, until Kent County Council claimed this was illegal and it was the far more restrictive Children and Young Persons Act which applied.

Now at the time of writing this ruling by Kent County Council has not been challenged in the courts, although Philip Circus, the legal adviser to the Incorporated Practitioners in Advertising, wrote in *Campaign* (22nd October 1983):

"The clear view among lawyers is that the definition of performance does not extend to still photography and that using child models in still photography is therefore technically illegal".

"Nevertheless, the authorities have largely turned a blind eye to the strict legal position. Generally speaking, providing there is no element of exploitation, local councils are not interested".

There the situation remains, and professional photographers who use child models could be at risk, although to quote Mr Circus again:

" . . . local authorities are unlikely to act except where a child's education is at risk. Quite apart from which, cuts in local government spending mean councils starting a list of priorities in law enforcement. The use of children in still photography is unlikely to be anywhere near the top".

Wildlife Photography

There is one field of photography which calls for specialised knowledge not only of the subject, but of the art of photography as well as the law. This is nature photography, particularly that part which concerns photographing birds and fledgelings in their nests.

Birds

Although it is not illegal to photograph rare breeding birds, to keep within the law a permit to do so must be obtained if the law contained in the Wildlife and Countryside Act 1981 is to be observed.

Basically, all wild birds, together with their eggs and nests, are protected, with the exception of the following thirteen which are referred to as pest species. These are:

Collared dove	Crow
Feral pigeon	Great black-backed gull
Herring gull	House sparrow
Jackdaw	Jay
Lesser black-backed gull	Magpie
Rook	Starling
Woodpigeon.	

The object of, in effect, prohibiting the photography of wild birds by anyone without a licence, is to prevent rare breeding species being disturbed on or near their nests. Licences may be obtained from the Nature Conservancy Council. The penalty for failing to have a licence is a fine of up to £1,000.

However, obtaining a licence is not an easy matter; the Nature Conservancy Council rightly will demand references as to the skill and expertise of the applicant before granting a licence for the first time. Thereafter, references may not be necessary. The following is the list of specially protected birds for which a licence is necessary if pictures are to be taken of them on or near the nest:

Wild birds specially protected at all times

Avocet
Barn owl
Bearded tit
Bee-eater
Bewick's swan
Bittern
Black-necked grebe
Black redstart
Black-tailed godwit
Black tern
Black-winged stilt
Bluethroat
Brambling
Cetti's warbler
Chough
Cirl bunting
Common quail
Common scoter
Corncrake
Crested tit
Crossbills (all species)
Dartford warbler
Divers (all species)
Dotterel
Fieldfare
Firecrest

Garganey
Golden eagle
Golden oriole
Goshawk
Green sandpiper
Greenshank
Gyr falcon
Harriers (all species)
Hobby
Honey buzzard
Hoopoe
Kentish plover
Kingfisher
Lapland bunting
Leach's petrel
Little bittern
Little gull
Little ringed plover
Little tern
Long-tailed duck
Marsh warbler
Mediterranean gull
Merlin
Osprey
Peregrine
Purple heron

Purple sandpiper
Red-backed shrike
Red kite
Red-necked phalarope
Redwing
Roseate tern
Ruff
Savi's warbler
Scarlet rosefinch
Scaup
Serin
Shorelark
Short-toed treecreeper
Slavonian grebe
Snow bunting
Snowy owl
Spoonbill
Spotted crake
Stone curlew
Temminck's stint

Velvet scoter
Whimbrel
White-tailed eagle
Whooper swan
Woodlark
Wood sandpiper
Wryneck

Wild birds
specially
protected
during the
close season
Goldeneye
Greylag goose
(in Outer Hebrides,
Caithness, Sutherland
and Wester Ross only)
Pintail

Animals, fish and insects

Similar restrictions apply to the following list of specially protected species of animals, fish and insects, and a licence must be obtained if any are to be photographed in their places of shelter:

Mammals
Bats, all 15 species
Bottle-nosed dolphin
Common dolphin
Common otter
Harbour (or common) porpoise
Red squirrel

Amphibians
Great crested (or warty) toad
Natterjack toad

Butterflies
Chequered skipper
Heath fritillary
Large blue
Swallowtail
Other insects
Field cricket
Mole cricket
Norfolk aeshna dragonfly
Rainbow leaf beetle
Wart-biter grasshopper

Reptiles
Sand lizard
Smooth snake
Fish
Barbot
Moths
Barberry carpet
Black veined
Essex emerald

New Forest burnet
Reddish buff
Spiders
Fen raft spider
Ladybird spider
Snails
Carthusian
Glutinous
Sandbowl

Plants

There are other laws to protect wildlife and the countryside, of which all photographers should be aware in case specially protected wild plants are picked or damaged during the course of outdoor photography. It is unnecessary to hold a licence to photograph them, but it is illegal to pick, uproot or destroy them without a licence, or even collect their flowers and seeds.

The following are specially protected wild plants:

Adder's tongue Spearwort   *Ranunculus ophioglossifolius*
Alpine Catchfly   *Lychnis alpina*
Alpine Gentian *Gentiana nivalis*
Alpine Sow-thistle   *Cicerbita alpina*
Alpine Woodsia   *Woodsia alpina*
Bedstraw Broomrape   *Orobanche caryophyllacea*
Blue Heath   *Phyllodoce caerulea*
Brown Galingale   *Cyperus fuscus*
Chedder Pink   *Dianthus gratianopolitanus*
Childling Pink   *Petrorhagia nanteuilii*
Diapensia   *Diapensia lapponica*
Dickie's Bladder-fern   *Cystopteris dickieana*
Downy Woundwort   *Stachys germanica*
Drooping Saxifrage   *Saxifraga cernua*
Early Spider-orchid   *Ophrys sphegodes*
Fen Orchid   *Liparis loeselii*
Fen Violet   *Viola persicifolia*
Field Cow-wheat   *Melampyrum arvense*

Field Eryngo *Eryngium campestre*
Field Wormwood *Artemisia campestris*
Ghost Orchid *Epipogium aphyllum*
Greater Yellow-rattle *Rhinanthus serotinus*
Jersey Cudweed *Gnaphalium luteoalbum*
Killarney Fern *Trichomanes speciosum*
Lady's slipper *Cypripedium calceolus*
Late Spider-orchid *Orhys fuciflora*
Least Lettuce *Lactuca saligna*
Limestone Woundwort *Stachys alpina*
Lizard Orchid *Himantoglossum hircinum*
Military Orchid *Orchis militaris*
Monkey Orchid *Orchis simia*
Norwegian Sandwort *Arenaria norvegica*
Oblong Woodsia *Woodsia ilvensis*
Oxtongue Broomrape *Orobanche loricata*
Perenial Knawel *Scleranthus perennis*
Plymouth Pear *Pyrus cordata*
Purple Spurge *Euphorbia peplis*
Red Helleborine *Cephalanthera rubra*
Ribbon-leaved Water-plantain *Alisma gramineum*
Rock Cinquefoil *Potentilla rupestris*
Rock Sea-lavender (two rare species)
Limonium paradoxum/Limonium recurvum
Rough Marsh-mallow *Althaea hirsuta*
Round-headed Leek *Allium sphaerocephalon*
Sea Knotgrass *Polygonum maritimum*
Sickle-leaved Hare's-ear *Bupleurum falcatum*
Small Alison *Alyssum alyssoides*
Small Hare's-ear *Bupleurum baldense*
Snowdon Lily *Lloydia serotina*
Spiked Speedwell *Veronica spicata*
Spring Gentian *Gentiana verna*
Starfruit *Damasonium alisma*
Starved Wood-sedge *Carex depauperata*
Teesdale Sandwort *Minuartia stricta*
Thistle Broomrape *Orobanche reticulata*

Triangular Club-rush   *Scirpus triquetrus*
Tufted Saxifrage   *saxifraga cespitosa*
Water Germander   *Teucrium scordium*
Whorled Solomon's-seal   *Polygonatum verticillatum*
Wild Cotoneaster   *Cotoneaster integerrimus*
Wild Gladiolus   *Gladiolus illyricus*
Wood Calamint   *Calamintha sylvatica*

Radio controlled equipment

It is also illegal to use cameras and accessories which are radio controlled, and to do so is an offence under the Wireless Telegraphy Act 1949, enforcement of which licences all radio controlled equipment. It is not sufficient to have radio controlled equipment licensed; the radio frequencies used have to be approved by the radio regulatory department and this approval is not easily obtained.

One of the reasons for the stringency of the regulations is the fear that in what are, today, very crowded airwaves, there may be interference to radio controlled model aircraft which are also subject to regulations, causing them to go out of control and cause injury or damage or, worse still, interference with the radio bands used by emergency services.

It is interesting to note that there appears to be no prohibition on selling radio controlled cameras and accessories; the prohibition is on their use without a licence. Photographers should always ask what frequencies are used by radio controlled equipment before buying any such item, and then check with the Department of Trade to ensure the frequency falls into one of those which can be licensed. The penalties under the Wireless Telegraphy Act for using unlicensed equipment is a fine of up to £1,000 and/or imprisonment of up to three months.

Bye-laws

There are many other places and circumstances where there may be a prohibition on photography; indeed, in some circumstances the ban may be enforced by bye-laws which provide for penal sanctions by way of a fine for breach of bye-laws. It is a wise precaution for photographers who may have doubts about whether or not photography is allowed, to make sufficient inquiries to ascertain the position.

CHAPTER NINE

Trespass and Privacy

Unlike the situation which obtains in the United States of America, while the law in this country recognises the right of individuals and companies to maintain the confidentiality of their business affairs, there is no right to privacy which is protected by law. Of course, there is no greater intruder into privacy than the camera, and this is particularly true today with the ever increasing sophistication of zoom lenses which enable a photographer to take photographs from a distance.

However, having said there is no specific law giving a person a right to privacy, there are a number of other laws which afford some protection.

Trespass

Earlier reference has been made to photographers not trespassing. Unauthorised entry on another person's land is a trespass and is actionable *per se*—it is not necessary for actual damage to be proved, although without loss or damage any damages awarded are likely to be nominal.

There are instances when photographers are given permission to go onto another's land to take photographs but become trespassers if, when asked to leave, they do not do so, and in those circumstances the landowner is entitled to use reasonable force to eject the trespasser.

Trespass *ab initio*

There are also occasions when a photographer is invited into a person's house or on his land for a specific purpose, and does something contrary to or in excess of that purpose. When this happens the photographer becomes what is known as a trespasser *ab initio*, another legal term which means from the beginning. In other words, an act contrary to the purpose for which the invitation to enter was given, may lead to a case of trespass.

It is media photographers who are most likely to find themselves guilty of trespassing *ab initio*. They are often invited into premises to discuss taking photographs of a particular individual or individuals who are currently newsworthy. If the particular person or persons refuse to be photographed, it is not unknown for a picture to be "snatched".

From that moment a photographer is a trespasser *ab initio:* he was invited onto premises to discuss the taking of photographs and for nothing else. The unauthorised taking of a photograph is sufficient to revoke the licence which a court would imply was granted to enter for the discussion. The licence is automatically revoked by the wrongful act, and the photographer becomes a trespasser from the time he entered.

However, it should be remembered that there is no right to confiscate the film in such circumstances, as the photographer—even when trespassing—retains copyright in the photographs and right to possession of the film.

Invasion of privacy

The question of trespass to land has already been dealt with, and some protection is afforded by the laws of defamation, criminal libel, confidentiality and copyright, although this protection can usually only be invoked after there has been an invasion of privacy.

In October 1981 The Law Commission, which was set up in 1965 by the then Government to promote law reform, published its report on the law as it affected breach of confidence, and in doing so looked at the position of privacy.

As long ago as July 1972, another Government appointed body, the Younger Committee on Privacy, rejected proposals that there should be a general remedy for the protection of privacy, but recommended new remedies to cover certain specific ways in which privacy could be invaded.

The committee envisaged a criminal offence of surreptitious surveillance which, presumably, would cover not only electronic eavesdropping but also long distance photography. Indeed, the committee at paragraph 565 of its report suggested a civil remedy for both overt and surreptitious surveillance if, in either case, such surveillance had been carried out with a technical device which, were it not for the device, would justify the person being watched in believing he had protected himself or his possessions from surveillance by overhearing or observation.

It is 17 years since the Younger Committee reported, and there has been no attempt by any Government—and none is foreseeable—to implement the recommendations, so it might be argued that for the present and near future there is likely to be no legislation enshrining the right to privacy and providing criminal and/or civil sanctions against those guilty of an invasion of privacy.

Consequently those who seek to enforce their right to privacy by use of other branches of the law face a difficult task, as was amply demonstrated in 1977 in *Bernstein v Skyviews & General*. The plaintiff, Lord Bernstein, claimed damages for trespass to his land from the defendants, a firm of aerial photographers. Lord Bernstein claimed that by flying at the height of 630 feet over his land to take pictures of his home there had been a trespass.

This claim failed: Mr Justice Griffiths, as he then was, held that an owner of land had, at common law, rights not only on and below his land, but also to the airspace above to such height as was necessary for his ordinary use and enjoyment of his land and anything on it.

However, the judge held that even if the plane had flown over it was too high to be considered to be trespassing, and in any case the Civil Aviation Act 1949 section 40(1) provided a defence to such a claim against the operators of aircraft where the height was reasonable.

The judge did say that constant surveillance from the air using photography might well be an actionable nuisance.

Actionable nuisance

It is well worth examining this proposition further, especially in view of the lengths that some professional photographers for newspapers and magazines have been reported to go in order to get intimate pictures of personalities relaxing.

Would it be an actionable nuisance if Photographer A staked out the house and grounds of a personality from afar, in order to obtain intimate candid camera style photographs with the aid of a long distance lens? It is arguable that the answer would be no, for the simple reason that the "victim" of this type of surveillance, for this is what in fact it is, would be unaware of it and would therefore suffer no damage.

On the other hand, if the person concerned knew he or she was under surveillance to such an extent that it rendered it impossible to enjoy the use and benefit of his or her land, it is arguable that a nuisance has been committed, as Mr Justice Griffiths suggested in Bernstein's Case.

Conspiracy

It is possible to carry this argument forward: If Photographer A is sent by a newspaper or magazine to carry out such a surveillance, and it results in a nuisance being committed on the lines suggested in the previous paragraph, are the photographer and the publication guilty of conspiracy?

Conspiracy is both a crime and a tort, and in this case as far as the latter is concerned involves two or more persons agreeing without lawful justification to cause wilful damage to another or to perform an unlawful act which results in damage. Undoubtedly nuisance is an unlawful act, and consequently, in the situation suggested in the previous paragraph, both photographer and publication could be guilty of conspiracy. The effect of such a finding in a civil court would undoubtedly mean the award of exemplary damages, heavier than might be usual, which would serve not only to mark the court's displeasure at the conduct of the defendants but also to deter others from acting in a like manner.

However if such a nuisance by surveillance was for the purpose of exposing crime or iniquity, the person concerned would be unsuccessful in bringing any action, on the grounds that no action follows base cause.

Confidentiality

Closely allied to privacy is confidentiality and, although there is no legislation as such which codifies the law in this respect, there is no doubt there is a body of case law upon which a claim for breach of confidence can easily be based.

What, in effect, is meant by confidentiality as far as the law is concerned, is that a person is entitled to protect his own legal secrets. This applies with equal force to business and trade secrets.

The photographer who is an employer, in whatever way, is entitled to expect that any information he either imparts to his staff or they gain during the course of their employment, should remain confidential. This is essential if a photographic studio or picture news agency is likely to suffer adversely as a result of an employee revealing information which could lead to financial loss.

In 1969 Mr. Justice Megarry, as he then was, laid down three essential planks on which an action for breach of confidence must have to be successful.

The first was that information which has been imparted to another person must have the necessary "quality of confidence". This is not difficult to understand. If the owner of a photographic studio who wished to expand his business and buy new premises, confides in his staff that although willing to pay £15,000 for the lease of new studios, he was only prepared to offer £12,000 in the first instance, and that staff member reveals, for any reason, that information to the person with whom his employer is negotiating with the result that £15,000 has to be paid, the employee is in breach of confidence.

A similar explanation would suffice to cover the second plank, that the information must have been imparted in circumstances imposing an obligation to keep the information confidential.

(This point can be underlined by the fact that if the information was gained by an employee during the course of his employment there is an implied obligation on an employee to keep his employer's trade secrets confidential).

The third plank is that there must be unauthorised use of that information to the detriment of the party who communicated it to another person in confidence. Obviously, in the example cited the detriment would be that the owner of the photographic studio would have no alternative but to pay the full £15,000, when he might have obtained the lease of new premises for less.

Publication of confidential information

News photographers can fall foul of the law of confidentiality if they photograph for the purpose of publication, or even for verification, any document which is the subject of confidence.

One example of this was the case in 1974 of *Distillers v Times Newspapers* which is perhaps better known as "the thalidomide case". Distillers was being sued by a number of children who suffered deformities as a result, it was alleged, of their mothers taking the drug thalidomide during pregnancy. During the course of legal proceedings between the children and Distillers, a number of documents of a confidential nature as far as Distillers was concerned were revealed to expert advisers of the children.

Some of these documents came into the hands of *The Sunday Times*, who were well aware of their source. Distillers were successful in arguing that as they were revealed as part of the legal process they were entitled to special protection, and sought an injunction preventing their use. They were successful.

It is also thought that had they been unsuccessful in the action, they would have sought a further injunction on the grounds of breach of copyright, and copyright is an important weapon in the armoury of those seeking to enforce confidentiality; especially when breach of confidence involves publication of documents which are subject to copyright.

There is no confidence in iniquity; in other words, if a person receives in conditions of confidentiality information regarding a proposed breach of the law there can be no confidential relationship.

One of the defences which would be open to a photographer who, during the course of employment or even otherwise, photographed documents, is the defence of public interest.

In a judgment of the House of Lords in *British Steel Corporation v Granada Television Ltd*, which followed the broadcast of a television programme which used documents which were confidential to British Steel, Lord Wilberforce referred to circumstances when it would be legitimate to disclose confidential information in the public interest. In his lordship's view this went beyond iniquity to misconduct generally.

Apart from seeking an injunction to prevent publication, a person who has been the victim of a breach of confidence can sue for damages and also an account of profit which may have been made out of use of the breach. Furthermore, if a photographer during the course of following his work induced someone to reveal a breach of confidence, that photographer and, vicariously his employer if he had one, could be liable in law for damages for inducing such breach.

In 1981 the Law Commission recommended that the present action for breach of confidence be abolished, and replaced by a statute creating a new cause of action for such a breach and codifying the law as it exists today. So far no steps have been taken to implement any of the recommendations the Law Commission put forward.

Restrictions on Crown and Government property

Restrictions also apply to commercial photography in Royal Parks, certain historical monuments, and Government offices, all of which come under the Department of the Environment. Those who wish to photograph in these places have to pay £25 for an annual permit, although any costs incurred by the Department in connection with photography, will also be charged. In certain circumstances the fee can be waived if the photographer is prepared to transfer copyright to the Crown. It should also be noted that props are not allowed to be used in Royal Parks.

No charge is made for news, travelogues, magazine and press facilities, amateur photographers and media students, or for children's schools and adult education programmes.

Private property open to the public

Restrictions may or may not be imposed on visitors to stately homes, circuses, concerts, sporting events, etc. Much depends on the views of the organisers, although as far as theatres are concerned, the question of copyright of the performance may also be a factor which has to be considered.

An admission ticket does not give a *carte blanche* to the purchaser. Purchase only implies a licence to enter either stately house or grounds, theatre or concert hall, racecourse or stadium where a sporting event is held, and nothing more. In many of these places notices are prominently exhibited banning photography. It does not matter for what reason those responsible for imposing the ban have taken the action they have; it is sufficient that they have the right to do so and they do not have to explain, yet alone justify, such a ban on photography.

As mentioned earlier, a person who buys a ticket to visit a stately home or a theatre, concert hall or stadia, has a licence only to go into the premises for the purpose for which the entry ticket was sold. Failure to observe a ban on photography means the photographer is in breach of the condition of entry and therefore becomes a trespasser *ab initio*.

Under such circumstances, those in authority are entitled to expel the photographer, although they should not use undue force in doing so, nor should they attempt to confiscate the film. If film is seized or destroyed, or if undue force is used, the photographer is entitled to take action for damages.

Infringement of photographic rights

There is also the further possibility that photographic rights have been granted to a particular photographer, most usually in return for a fee or a share of the proceeds on any sale of photographs.

There is always the possibility that if the photographer who has been granted sole rights to take photographs at a certain function becomes aware of unauthorised photography by another, he would ask for, and in all probability be granted, an injunction restraining the other photographer from publishing unauthorised photographs.

CHAPTER TEN

Injury Risks

All photographers, whether they be amateurs or professionals, will from time to time expose themselves to physical harm for the sake of obtaining a better photograph. Instances when the risk of injury or even death could face a photographer are too numerous to enumerate, and even if they were listed they would not be exclusive.

In many instances a photographer who takes a risk may do so in a situation where only he is involved; there are other occasions where third parties are involved, and this could undoubtedly cause legal problems and even lead to litigation.

Injury to photographers

In previous chapters the question of trespass by photographers has been discussed. It is not at all unlikely that a photographer is trespassing at the time he sustains an injury.

The fact that he is a trespasser does not necessarily preclude him from bringing a claim for damages, although it is likely to be strenuously resisted.

Unless the landowner deliberately set out to injure a photographer who was trespassing, it is very doubtful that a photographer would recover damages for injuries sustained.

One must therefore look primarily at those situations where injury is caused to a photographer who is not a trespasser; when he is invited into premises or onto land, an obligation is placed on the owners to ensure the safety of the photographer and, of course, such an obligation extends to all owners or occupiers of land.

An important, indeed major, piece of legislation in this field is The Occupiers' Liability Act 1957, which lays a common duty of care on all occupiers as far as lawful visitors to their premises are concerned. That duty is to take such care as, in all the circumstances, is necessary to ensure the visitor is reasonably safe in using the premises for the purpose of which he has been invited to enter or permitted to be there.

Photographic studios

As far as those readers who own photographic studios are concerned, potential customers, or photographic sundries salesmen, have implied permission to enter.

One section of the Act, 2(1), allows an occupier to restrict or exclude his liability, but as photographic studios would be classified as business premises, consideration must be given to the Unfair Contract Terms Act 1977, which states that the common duty of care in regard to liability for injury or death cannot be excluded. It is worthwhile noting at this juncture that the same Act permits exclusion of liability for damage or other loss on business premises only where such exclusion is reasonable.

Awareness of risks

For the purpose of the photographer who enters premises, with consent, in pursuit of photographs, the occupier is entitled to assume that the photographer is aware of any risks he may be taking. For example, a photographer taking photographs of an old building which may have some unsafe features about it, may find himself met with the defence of *volenti non fit injuria* if he sues for any injuries sustained.

Freely translated this means that injury is not done to a man who knew of the risk and accepted it. Even if the defence of *volenti* is either not raised or is pleaded unsuccessfully, there is always the possibility of a judge finding the photographer was guilty of contributory negligence, and reducing the damages according to what percentage of fault lay with the photographer himself.

Sporting events

The risk of injury to a photographer is likely at sporting events, and this is a contentious area. A leading case in this field involved a press photographer who was injured while covering a horse show (*Wooldridge v Sumner, 1962*). The photographer was unfamiliar with horses and had, in fact, ignored the request of a steward to move outside the competition area. The photographer's claim for damages for negligence on the part of the rider was successful, but the Court of Appeal reversed the decision.

The Court of Appeal held that negligence had not been established, and Lord Justice Diplock went on to lay down certain principles of particular interest to photographers taking pictures at sporting events.

Lord Justice Diplock said: "If, in the course of a game or competition, at a moment when he has not time to think, a participant by mistake takes a wrong measure he is not to be held guilty of negligence".

The learned judge went on: "A person attending a game or competition takes the risk of any damage caused to him by any act of a participant done in the course of and for the purposes of the game or competition, notwithstanding that such act may involve an error of judgement or a lapse of skill, unless the participant's conduct is such to evince a reckless disregard of the spectator's safety.

"The spectator takes the risk because such an act involves no breach of the duty of care owed by the participant to him. He does not take the risk by virtue of the doctrine expressed or obscured by the maxim *Volenti non fit injuria* . . . the consent that is relevant is not consent to the risk of injury but consent to the lack of reasonable care that may produce that risk".

Another judgement which underlined that of Lord Justice Diplock, was given in the Court of Appeal some nine years later. In this case—*Wilks v Cheltenham Home Guard Motor Cycle and Light Car Club*—two spectators sued for injuries sustained at a motor cycle scramble, which they were watching from a roped off enclosure. A competitor left the course and crashed through the enclosure injuring them.

The Court of Appeal held that the rider had not been negligent, and it was to have been expected that at such an event loss of control could occur.

In its judgement the Court of Appeal said a competitor must use reasonable care, but this meant reasonable care having regard to the fact that, as a competitor, he was expected to go all out to win and expected to go as fast as he could as long as he was not foolhardy.

On these two cases alone it can be seen the risk photographers run of failing in an action for damages should they be injured while photographing sporting events.

Injury to third parties

Similar considerations would apply also to claims in respect of photographic equipment.

A photographer like any other citizen owes a reasonable duty of care to those he is likely to come across during the taking of photographs. Unfortunately it is not possible to state categorically what that care should be.

Each case must depend upon its own merits but a practical guideline would be to say that a photographer should do nothing which is likely to cause harm to a person or property. It is advisable that this is remembered when using flashlight equipment, as there are circumstances where the sudden and unexpected use of a flash could lead to a person being injured as a result of the flash unsettling them, or a horse, if engaged in some form of activity. There is little doubt that a court would hold the photographer responsible in law for any subsequent injury.

Liability of photographers and their employers

In considering liability for injury caused as a result of a photographer taking pictures, there is another important factor to be taken into consideration: this is whether or not the photographer is an employed person. If an amateur or a freelance, the photographer is solely liable in damages.

If employed, the employer may well be vicariously liable, and both photographer and employer would be joined in any action for damages. It is therefore necessary to examine what, in law, constitutes an employed person, as this can have important repercussions as far as the freelance photographer who has been commissioned to undertake a specific assignment is concerned.

One of the leading legal textbook writers on the subject suggests that a servant—that is, an employed person—can be defined as any person employed by another to do work for him on terms that he, the servant, is to be subject to the control and direction of his employer in respect of the manner in which his work is to be done.

Usually an employer–servant relationship can now be determined by the existence of a contract of service, which all employees have to receive within thirteen weeks of taking up employment. Such a contract usually lays down conditions of employment and other relevant matters. On the other hand, a freelance photographer may have a contract for service with a particular newspaper. This may be a contract to undertake a specific assignment, or even to be a permanent casual working a specified number of days a week.

I would hope that no newspaper which has a contract for service would hide behind this to seek to avoid vicarious liability, but if this is the case, the courts apply a further test to determine whether a master–servant relationship exists, and that is who has right of control over the person carrying out the work.

Originally, such right of control was held to mean the right of an employer to tell his employee how the work was to be done. Today this would be unrealistic, especially with competent professional freelance photographers. Consequently this test has been modified and courts now tend to look for who has control to such matters as number of hours to be worked and where they are to be worked, and in the case of a freelance photographer doing casual work, the right of the newspaper or magazine to select photographic assignments for that person to do during hours of work.

Once an employer–employee relationship has been established, a photographer who has caused injury should be covered under the Employers' Liability (Compulsory Insurance) Act 1969, as far as injuries to colleagues are concerned, but there is no compulsory cover in respect of injuries to others who are not colleagues. However, this is likely to be covered under the employer's public liability policy.

Freelance photographers should, in their own interest, get public liability coverage if they do not hold it already.

PART II

So far this book has dealt solely with the law as it affects a photographer in actually carrying out photography, and this has pre-supposed that the photographer has the necessary equipment and, if not a serious amateur, is in business as either a freelance or the principal of a studio, or as a professional photographer in full time employment.

The remainder of the book will be devoted to the rights and obligations of the photographer as an employer, employee, consumer or user of services. There are no special rights as far as a photographer is concerned in these subjects. He has the same rights, no more and no less, as any other citizen and, like his fellow man in the street, is probably only dimly aware of what those rights are.

As Lord Young of Dartington says in his preface to *A Handbook of Consumer Law:* "It is important that consumers should know their law and use their knowledge to good effect. Moreover, self-interest combines with altruism. Anyone who stands up for his rights is also helping to protect everyone else's. Rights can rust unless they are used".

CHAPTER ELEVEN

Purchase of Equipment

Photographic equipment can be cheap or expensive. Whatever the price, the same consumer legislation applies, though serious amateurs or professional photographers are more likely to purchase cameras and accessories at the top end of the market to enable then to take better pictures. Consequently, they should be more aware of their rights as a consumer because of the greater financial outlay.

The purchaser's best protection is to be found in The Sale of Goods Act 1979, which replaced an Act of the same title passed in 1893.

Control of sale

Before going into greater detail it must be remembered that any purchase is a contract; a simple contract, yes, but a contract nonetheless. It means, as far as purchases are concerned, that the seller offers goods at a certain price to a potential buyer. The buyer can make up his or her own mind whether or not to accept the goods at the stated price. If he does, a binding contract is entered into between buyer and seller. Such a contract is equally binding whether it is a verbal agreement or a written one.

As far as the purchase of photographic equipment is concerned, the consumer can look to Section 14(2) of the 1979 Act for protection. This section reads:

"Where the seller sells goods in the course of a business there is an implied condition that goods supplied under the contract are of merchantable quality, except that there is no such condition (a) as regards defects specifically drawn to the buyer's attention before the contract is made, or (b) if the buyer examines the goods before the contract is made, as regards defects which that examination ought to reveal".

Section 14(6) states: "goods of any kind are of merchantable quality ... if they are as fit for the purpose or purposes for which goods of that kind are commonly bought as it is reasonable to expect having regard to any description applied to them, the price (if relevant) and all other relevant circumstances".

Finally, Section 61(1) of the Act says that the word quality in relation to goods includes their state or condition.

This means that a photographer who buys a camera or any piece of equipment is entitled to expect it to be reasonably fit for its normal purpose and free from defects. If the casing of a camera is damaged or marked in some way it may not be of merchantable quality, at least at the price which is demanded. However, the photographer who accepts the camera having had such a defect pointed out to him, or having been given the opportunity to inspect it, has no comeback. He is deemed to have accepted the article when he was aware, or should have been aware and would have been if he had inspected it, of the defect.

On the other hand, the buyer of a camera or accessory which is defective in its actual mechanism, which could not be seen without taking it apart, has a piece of equipment which is definitely not of merchantable quality.

Equipment must also be fit for the purpose for which it was bought if the particular reason for which the equipment is required is made known to the seller. Consequently, a photographer who asks for a camera or accessory with the capacity to do certain tasks, and is sold one which does not measure up to his requirements, can demand his money back.

Such a demand for monetary refund must be made as soon as is reasonably possible after a defect is discovered, or the buyer realises he has not got what he wanted. Bear in mind, however, that merchantable quality and fitness for purpose may often depend upon what is considered customary for a particular piece of equipment.

The two conditions—merchantable quality and fitness for purpose—are what the law calls 'implied terms' in all sales, and there is a third term which is contained in Section 13 of the Act. This is that goods must fit their description, which must be as described either orally by a salesman or in writing on a package.

These conditions, upon which consumers are entitled to rely, do not apply to goods sold by a person who is not in business selling the particular line of goods. Thus, a photographer who buys equipment from someone who is not in the photographic business, or from a private person, will only have a claim on the ground of misrepresentation, a subject which is dealt with later.

The "Photocode"

Fortunately, most reputable photographic dealers operate what is called the "Photocode", a code of practice which has been drawn up by a number of trade associations within the photographic industry in conjunction with the Office of Fair Trading.

The trade associations which subscribe to the code are:

Association of British Manufacturers of Photographic, Cine and Audio-Visual Equipment;
Association of Photographic Laboratories;
British Institute of Professional Photography;
British Photographic Association;
British Photographic Importers Association;
Institute of Photographic Apparatus Repair Technicians;
Master Photographers' Association;
National Pharmaceutical Association; and
Professional Photographic Laboratories Association.

There was a further and very important body which subscribed originally to the code, the Photographic Dealers Association, which offered a facility for conciliation in respect of complaints against one of its members. Unfortunately the association has gone out of business, but the subscribers named above have agreed to continue their support, and complaints which cannot be resolved by a dealer or the relevant manufacturer or importer can be referred to the appropriate trade body.

Rights of the purchaser

What does the law offer to the genuinely dissatisfied consumer? The three implied terms of any sale contained in the Sale of Goods Act 1979 are as we know, that the goods should fit their description, be of merchantable quality, and fit for their purpose.

If goods fail to measure up to any of these three criteria the consumer is entitled to ask for his money back; he is not obliged to settle for a replacement or a repair.

There are, however, circumstances where defective goods can be kept and part of the money paid refunded, the sum paid being the difference between the value of the goods without the defect and the value with the defect. In Scotland, where the law is different, it is more than probable that a replacement can be insisted upon.

Do not be fobbed off with a credit note offered by a shop. In law, a consumer who has purchased defective goods or goods which are not fit for their purpose is entitled to a monetary refund and not a credit note.

The same applies to guarantees. They are useful in as much as they give a consumer the knowledge that if, during the period of the guarantee— usually 12 months in the case of new items—repairs are necessary, such repairs will be carried out by skilled craftsmen using proper materials and component parts.

But if a camera or other accessory proves to be seriously defective within a short time of purchase, it must be remembered that a contract exists between consumer and seller; not consumer and manufacturer, unless purchased directly from the maker. Legally the manufacturer is not a party to the contract, and the purchaser of defective goods need not rely on the guarantee but can enforce his rights against the dealer. The dealer has the same rights *vis-a-vis* the manufacturer.

Consequential loss

There is also the possibility that a piece of defective equipment could result in what the law terms consequential loss or damage. This is restricted, however, to loss or damage which may fairly and reasonably be considered as arising naturally and in the usual course of things from the defect. The right to claim for consequential loss or damage is additionally restricted, in as much as a complainant must prove that such a loss or damage could be within the contemplation of the dealer.

This is restrictive because otherwise every seller would be at risk if damage was caused. To give an example: if a flash gun was so seriously defective as to explode injuring the user, this would, it could be submitted, be something which a dealer could reasonably contemplate happening if there was an explosion due to an integral defect.

In such circumstances, the photographer could bring an action against the dealer not only for a breach of the implied terms that the flash gun was of merchantable quality, but also for the consequential damage it caused. It is more than probable that, in those circumstances, the dealer would look to the manufacturer to cover himself from any financial loss.

Exclusion clauses

From time to time written contracts of sale, guarantees, etc., contain an exclusion or exemption clause, a notice which purports to deny the consumer some of his rights as far as the trader is concerned.

Such clauses may take many forms; some may disclaim any responsibility for any loss or damage, although this will apply to services which are dealt with later; others will seek to substitute any statutory rights in favour of those rights, which are usually restrictive, granted by a guarantee. Fortunately, not only are reputable dealers not using these doubtful practices, they are also subject to the stringent conditions of the Supply of Goods (Implied Terms) Act 1973 and the Unfair Contract Terms Act 1977.

As a result of these items of legislation, no guarantee or contract for sale can validly exclude a traders basic liability under the Sale of Goods Act, or liability for negligence causing death or injury.

Not only that; if a trader wishes to exclude liability under the Misrepresentation Act 1967, which applies only to England and Wales or the Misrepresentation Act (Northern Ireland) 1967, the trader has to prove such exclusion was reasonable.

Normally, guarantees today state that nothing contained in such documents affect the purchaser's statutory rights; indeed, any guarantee which omits such a declaration could result in the firm which produced it being prosecuted, as it is illegal under the Consumer Transactions (Restrictions on Statements) Order 1976 and Amendment Order 1978, and the maker(s) of such statements can be prosecuted.

In all transactions where there are exemption or exclusion clauses, the test the courts apply is one of reasonableness, and the onus is on the person seeking to avoid liability by hiding behind the clause to prove it was reasonable. To succeed in doing so, it will be necessary to prove such a clause was fair and reasonable in the circumstances of the particular transaction, the circumstances of which were, or ought to have been, reasonably known to, or likely to be considered by, both parties to the contract. One of the main items a court will look at is the bargaining position of both parties.

If the trader who is seeking to enforce the exemption clause was in a stronger position than his customer, he is not likely to be able to seek refuge in the clause.

It is worth reiterating that on the whole those who deal in cameras and photographic accessories are reputable. Unfortunately not all assistants who work in shops, stores, etc., are as aware of consumer rights as their employers are. In such circumstances, the employer is liable, although ignorance on the part of an assistant may be a mitigating factor as far as an offence of a criminal nature is concerned, but not in any claim for damages.

Misrepresentation

Ignorance, sometimes on the part of a proprietor, but most likely on the part of an assistant, may lead to misrepresentations being made about cameras or photographic equipment. Such statements are covered by the Misrepresentation Act 1967 which does not apply to Scotland where, however, the existing law is very similar.

There are three main forms of misrepresentation—innocent, negligent and fraudulent. An innocent misrepresentation occurs when the seller makes a statement about goods which he believes to be true at the time, and as a result of which a buyer enters into a contract to purchase.

Negligent misrepresentation takes place when a seller makes a claim for goods for which he has no reasonable grounds to believe is true. This entitles the purchaser to compensation in England and Wales, and it is only necessary to prove that such a negligent misrepresentation was made; in

Scotland it is necessary to prove not only that a misrepresentation was made, but it was made negligently—a much higher standard.

Fraudulent misrepresentation means a deliberately untrue statement, and this would arise if a salesman lied about the capacity of a particular camera a potential purchaser was interested in buying. Compensation for such fraudulent misrepresentation can be obtained if it is too late to rescind the contract.

Furthermore, if as a result of such a fraudulent misrepresentation the photographer incurred expense in seeking to take photographs which were beyond the technical capacity of the camera, he is entitled to damages by way of compensation for any loss suffered as a result of reliance on the fraudulent statement.

It must be remembered, however, that for a disgruntled consumer to rely on the Misrepresentation Act a misrepresentation must refer to the past or the present, not the future. So in the example cited in the previous paragraph, if the salesman said he had used a particular camera for a type of photography with good results, this would be sufficient to prove misrepresentation; on the other hand, if he said he believed a particular camera would be capable of taking certain types of photographs, there would be no misrepresentation, because not only would such a claim refer to a future event, it would also be a statement of opinion not of fact.

In all cases of misrepresentation it is essential that any claim upon which a case stands or falls must be one of fact and not of opinion.

One other piece of legislation worth noting is The Trades Description Act 1968, which makes it a criminal offence for a trader to misrepresent goods or a service. Complaints have to be made to the local trading standards office, who have discretion on whether or not to prosecute.

As far as the consumer is concerned, a prosecution does not necessarily mean that he will be compensated for any loss incurred as a result of a misdescription. Magistrates hearing the case do have power to order compensation, but do not always do so. However, a conviction under the Trades Description Act is most persuasive in a subsequent claim for compensation in a county court.

Hire purchase and credit sales

Many photographers buy their more expensive equipment on hire purchase. This is an agreement which is legally binding, and by which the goods are hired to the buyer with an option to buy for a nominal sum, usually £1, at the end of the hire period. Any person who has bought equipment in this manner cannot sell it without the consent of the hirer.

Then there is a credit sale, which is similar to a hire purchase agreement except the goods become the property of the purchaser immediately. One of the major pieces of legislation controlling sales in which credit is involved is the Consumer Credit Act 1974, which extends the protection given by the Hire Purchase Act 1965.

If the amount of credit involved is between £50 and £5,000, the agreement must be in writing, and the creditor must be given a copy which must also state what is the rate of interest charged.

Many purchases are now made by credit cards issued by banks, and again these are controlled by the Consumer Credit Act. Nevertheless, whatever form of credit is granted to allow a buyer to purchase goods does not in any way take away rights as far as The Sale of Goods Act is concerned.

Having been granted credit there is a legal obligation on the borrower to repay the loan, and failure to do so can lead to an action, usually in a county court. Dependant upon the amount of the debt, the goods can be repossessed, but usually only with a County Court order.

In today's economic climate, those who grant credit are usually sympathetic to the borrower who falls on hard times, provided that the changed circumstances are made known to the lender as soon as possible. In most cases of genuine hardship, lenders are willing to reduce the monthly payments, or accept an interest only payment leaving the balance to be paid off when the borrower is in a better financial position. A condition would be that any change in financial circumstances of the hirer is made known to the finance company immediately.

CHAPTER TWELVE

Photographic Services

Today nothing poses more problems to photographers than the services they receive or, perhaps to be more accurate, do not receive from the numerous firms offering developing and printing. One of the main problems concerns exemption or exclusion clauses, which were referred to in the previous chapter.

Exclusion clauses in D & P

In most cases such a clause is likely to be expressed in the following terms: "Whilst every care is taken of film(s), prints and negatives our responsibility for lost or damaged films is limited to the cost of the unexposed film and the processing charge". Sometimes such exclusion clauses may contain the expression "even if our fault", but the result is still the same.

This exclusion clause was challenged some years ago, by a photographer who submitted to a firm offering a developing and printing service, a roll of film he had taken of a friend's wedding. It was his intention to present them in an album as a wedding present to his friend.

The case was first heard using the arbitration method available in county courts for small claims, and the photographer was awarded £75 compensation. The firm appealed against the award, but Judge Clarke sitting in Exeter County Court upheld the arbitration findings.

As was mentioned in the last chapter, it was not until 1977 that the Unfair Contract Terms Act was passed, which laid down that exclusion clauses would only be upheld by the courts if they were fair and reasonable in all circumstances. In the Exeter case, Judge Clarke held the clause to be unfair and unreasonable, and while this was a major step forward as far as a consumer's rights was concerned, it did not create a precedent. The decision is not binding, and consequently a judge might take a different view on another occasion.

The Supply of Goods and Services Act

In July 1983, a section of the Supply of Goods and Services Act 1982 came into law which laid down three criteria that those who supply services must follow: the work must be carried out with reasonable care and skill; within a reasonable time unless the contrary is agreed; and at a reasonable charge.

There is little doubt that if a photographer brought an action against a developing and printing firm, the first hurdle the firm would have to overcome would be in proving the exclusion clause was fair and reasonable in all the circumstances. Strange to say, one of the points which might well be taken into consideration in deciding whether this point had been established, would be the size of the small print. The smaller the print, and therefore the greater difficulty a consumer would have in reading it, might well result in the clause being held to be unreasonable.

Other circumstances would also be considered, of which the most important would be the bargaining position of the two parties. Most, if not all, of the major firms offering developing and printing services by post carry exclusion clauses, and this would in all probability be a point in favour of a photographer, as it would mean he was unable to avoid making use of this type of firm. If there were developing and printing firms in his locality, or within a short distance, which offered a comparable service but without the disclaimer of responsibility for loss or damage, there would be a competent alternative for a photographer to use. This being unavailable, it is most likely that the strong bargaining position of the developing and printing firm was such that an exclusion clause would be held unreasonable.

Undoubtedly a firm which either loses or damages prints and negatives is not carrying out the service with reasonable care and skill.

Assessing damages

There is a great difference between establishing liability and gaining an award of damages of greater value than the replacement of the ruined roll of film. To understand why, it is necessary to understand that the concept of an award of damages is not to enrich victims of negligence, but put them in the position they would have been in but for the damage caused.

Consequently one must ask how can damages be quantified for a lost or damaged roll of film? Many of the complaints which follow as a result of lost or damaged film refer to pictorial records of holidays or special family events being spoiled by the negligence of the developing and printing firm.

The question to be asked is this: did the negligence spoil the holiday or family celebration? Common sense dictates that the answer must be no, because, at the time of the holiday or family celebration, the question of the future negligence of the developing and printing firm did not arise. This was a *post facto* occurrence which by no conceivable stretch of the imagination could be held to have spoiled the event.

On the other hand, a photographer who sets out on a specific photographic mission with, say, the sole intention of capturing on film the Pyramids or the Taj Mahal, could have a claim. The strength of such a claim would depend on one main factor; could the developing and printing firm have reasonably foreseen the loss which would follow from its negligence?

The answer must be, again, no. Any firm which receives either through the post or over the counter, either directly at its own premises or through an agent, is in no position to know whether a roll of film depicts the Pyramids or the Taj Mahal, to get pictures of which the photographer has gone to considerable expense—or just back yard snapshots.

The argument would be equally valid if the films were given to a photographic studio to process by hand and were lost or damaged.

Precautions against loss or damage

In such circumstances the photographer should declare in writing what the contents of the film are, and state the expense involved in getting the particular shots, thus putting the developing and printing firm on notice that there was a high cost factor involved in obtaining the photographs. If the photographer had been commissioned to take the particular photographs, the value of that commission should also be made known to the firm.

Otherwise any claim for loss of earnings would be met by the perfectly reasonable defence that the firm was unable to reasonably foresee that there was commercial value in the film.

Many firms offering development and printing services now display in a prominent position a warning that if film to be developed has a value over and above the nominal sum usually paid if something goes wrong in the D & P process, this should be stated at the time the film is handed in for developing.

In some instances a small additional charge is made which, presumably, is a form of insurance premium to indemnify the photographer against financial loss. While this may be a step in the right direction, the onus is still on the photographer to take this step and pay extra, when it should be on the developer and printer to ensure that loss is not suffered as a result of negligence.

This uncertainty over what recompense, if any, a photographer may expect to receive for films lost or damaged, causes great concern to serious amateurs and professional photographers who may have invested large sums of money to get a certain set of photographs.

Although it is arguable that developing and printing firms should carry sufficient insurance to meet genuine claims, that does not appear to be the position today. It could be that if a precedent was set by a decision in either the Queens Bench Division of the High Court, the Court of Appeal, or even the House of Lords, which placed responsibility for loss or damage squarely upon firms, that steps to introduce a system of insurance would follow in a very short time.

Insurance of films

Until then, the photographer who wishes to protect his investment in taking photographs must insure them himself. From time to time complaints are received by those deeply involved in the photographic field, that it is difficult to obtain a policy to cover all eventualities.

This may well be the case with ordinary companies, but there are many syndicates of underwriters at Lloyd's of London who take on all types of risk. Photographers seeking to cover themselves should contact a broker and get a policy specially written to cover any losses. In doing so, it will be necessary to specify the costs involved or likely to be involved in obtaining the photographs.

However it is important for photographers negotiating either annual cover or an ad hoc policy to reduce to writing the risks to be covered, and this is dealt with in greater detail in Chapter 15.

Equipment repairs and servicing

There is one other aspect of the Supply of Goods and Services Act 1982 which affects photographers, and this is repairs and servicing of equipment. Under the Act repairs and servicing have to be carried out with reasonable care and skill; of course this leads to the inevitable question of the standard of reasonableness.

As far as reputable photographic dealers who offer to undertake repairs and servicing are concerned, there is no doubt the standard of reasonable care would be held to be that which a trained and competent service engineer, properly supervised, should bring to a particular task.

Failure to exercise that degree of care and skill could lead to the dissatisfied photographer claiming damages. There is no doubt he could recover the costs of the repair or service which was not carried out with the necessary care and skill but again, the question to be asked is this:

What damage flows from the failure to exercise that care and skill?

The same considerations would apply as to the film ruined in the developing and printing process.

Although it may seem an unnecessary and pedantic step, a photographer seeking a repair or service of his camera before setting out to capture on film some specific place or event which involves expense, should state this fact to the person accepting the repair or service. That person is then on notice that failure to carry out the repair or service properly, could lead to the photographer being out of pocket as a result.

More important from the legal point of view, the service engineer is aware that failure to carry out the necessary work could result in financial loss to the customer. In other words, he has knowledge of loss which could result, and cannot argue that he could not reasonably expect to foresee consequential loss.

Similar considerations apply to the question of the time the repair or service takes. The Act states that work shall be carried out within a reasonable time, unless the contrary is agreed. Again, the yardstick is what is a "reasonable time". Undoubtedly the skill and competence of those offering the service would be considered, as would the time of the year, if it can be shown that certain times are much busier than others.

Usually service engineers will state how long work will take, and it is up to the photographer to accept this estimate or find someone else who will do it quicker. If a photographer convinces a service engineer that it is important for the work to be completed within a specified time, and the engineer agrees to carry out the work in that time, a contract has been entered into in which time is of the essence. Failure on the part of the engineer to carry out the work within the specified time is a breach of contract. This gives the photographer the opportunity to rescind the contract and in some circumstances, claim damages; but again, it is necessary to prove the engineer could foresee, or be reasonably expected to foresee, that damage would flow.

Under the new Act, charges must be reasonable: perhaps this is the easiest part of this particular section of the Act to quantify. The service engineer would have to prove his charge was reasonable.

This would be done by proving the hourly rate charged was consistent with that charged by other engineers in the area, that any parts replaced were within the manufacturers price guide and, if any profit margin was added to cover other overheads, this was not outrageously high.

The new legislation is an important weapon in the armoury of consumer law, as it codifies what can be legally expected from those who provide services. Unfortunately, claims under the Act are likely to be small and therefore dealt with by county courts, where any finding of liability on the part of a supplier of services, although persuasive, is not binding as a High Court judgement would be.

CHAPTER THIRTEEN

Employment Law

Although the object of this book is to inform all photographers of their legal rights and obligations, it is hoped that it will be of particular help to those who take photographs for a living, either on their own account, as an employee, or as semi-professionals who use photography not only as a satisfying hobby but also one which is financially beneficial.

This chapter will deal with the question of employment law, and explain the law from the viewpoint of both employer and employee.

Contracts of employment

From the time an employee is engaged, both sides are entering into a contractual obligation. It is essential that both employer and employee have a clear understanding of their positions *vis-a-vis* employment, and as a starting point it is necessary to look at the Employment Protection (Consolidation) Act 1978. This places an obligation on an employer to give employees, within 13 weeks of starting work, a written statement setting out conditions of employment. This statement must contain the hours to be worked, pay and methods of payment, as well as any other conditions of employment. Information must also be given about holiday pay and entitlement, sickness pay, if any, and any pension benefits.

The contract of employment can be more important for a professional photographer than most other employees, for it is in this contract that any restrictions on work outside his employment have to be stated.

For the photographer employed in newspapers, magazines or other branches of the media, disputes often arise as to who owns copyright of photographs taken outside of working hours. Assuming an employed photographer takes photographs outside his working hours using his own camera and film, copyright in those photographs should be his. As far as the law of copyright is concerned it is; on the other hand, the contract of service may well give copyright to the employer even if such photographs are taken outside of normal working hours.

Dismissal

It is when the time comes for an employee to be dismissed or made redundant that it is necessary for both employer and employee to be aware of legal pitfalls. Every employee who has worked continuously for 26 weeks has to be given a written statement outlining the reason for dismissal. If the employee has worked for more than 52 consecutive weeks there is a legal right not to be dismissed unfairly. In the case of a firm which employs fewer than 20 staff, this right exists after 102 consecutive weeks of work.

Many photographic studios employ part time workers, and the conditions in the previous paragraph apply to part timers who, in the past five consecutive years, have worked between eight and sixteen hours a week.

In giving an employee notice it is crucial that the period stated in the contract of service be honoured, and if no duration of notice is stated the custom of the trade is observed. It is also generally accepted that a weekly paid photographer is entitled to a week's notice unless the contract of service states differently.

An employee on a fixed term contract may have a claim for unfair dismissal if the contract is not extended when it expires, unless the employer writes into the contract—and the employee accepts—a clause which precludes him from complaining of unfair dismissal.

Unfair dismissal

It was in 1971 that unfair dismissal was introduced as a legal concept into employment law: unfair dismissal means that every employee has the legal right not to be dismissed unfairly either with or without notice. There is also another category of dismissal which is known as constructive dismissal. This follows when an employer repudiates one of the conditions of employment contained in the contract of service, and as a result of such behaviour an employee leaves.

There are five grounds for dismissal that the law regards as fair:

Lack of capability or qualification on the part of an employee to do the job for which they were engaged;
Misconduct;
When continued employment would be breach of the law;
Redundancy;
Other substantial reasons.

Obviously little explanation is required for the first two reasons, although it must be remembered that the longer an incompetent employee is allowed to continue in employment, the more difficult it is for the employer to legally dismiss him on grounds of incompetence.

Misconduct would cover not only recognisable criminal offences like theft from the employer but, in the case of a photographer, undertaking photographic work either in defiance of a contractual ban against doing so, or poaching his employer's clients in order to carry out work on a freelance basis.

The third ground, when continued employment would be a breach of the law, is only likely to affect a photographer for whom it is essential that he can drive to carry out assignments. Loss of his driving licence would mean that he could no longer go out on assignments where public transport was not available, and driving while disqualified is a criminal offence.

Redundancy

With redundancy, the greatest care has to be taken by the employer to ensure that the dismissed employee is, in fact, really redundant. In the past, employers have tried to get rid of unwanted workers by seeking to clothe dismissal with the cloak of redundancy.

It is important that an employer warns an employed photographer of possible redundancy as far ahead as possible. If there are ten or less employees to be dismissed on the grounds of redundancy, consultation with an independent trade union recognised by the employer must take place at the earliest practicable opportunity. Although it is unlikely to affect many employers in a small way of business, if the number of employees to be made redundant is between 10 and 99, the Department of Employment must be informed at least 30 days before dismissals become effective. If redundancies are to total more than 100, both the Department of Employment and any unions must be informed at least 90 days before dismissals come into force.

There are a number of considerations to be weighed in the balance as far as redundancy is concerned, and it matters not whether one or 101 employees are declared redundant. Obviously there are some guidelines, and they are as follows:

If all or part of an employer's business closes;
The business moves its location;
The business is sold; and
The employee(s) is put on part time or laid off.

Complications can and frequently do arise when a business moves. If a photographer is not offered another job at the new site he is legally redundant. However, if he is offered a job which for family and/or financial reasons he cannot take up because of the move of the business, redundancy can only be claimed if there is not a mobility clause in the photographer's contract of service. Such a clause will stipulate that if a photographic—or any other business—moves, the employee will move with it. If a photographer accepts such a clause and then chooses not to move, he cannot claim to have been made redundant, for there is a job available for him within the same business.

Even in the absence of such a mobility clause, a photographer could still find it difficult to mount successfully a claim for redundancy. In the absence of a mobility clause an industrial tribunal, hearing a case for unfair dismissal, will look at all the circumstances of the individual case before arriving at a decision.

If a reallocation of work or a change in work methods results in the need of fewer staff so that some employees are not needed, those employees are redundant. But if, as a result of working methods, an employee is asked to do a different shift and he chooses not to accept, he is most unlikely to succeed in a claim for redundancy. On the other hand, if imposition of new working hours results in a breach on the part of the employer of the contract of service between him and the employee, the employee may well succeed in a claim for redundancy payments.

When a business is sold and the staff dismissed, redundancy payments must be made, but if sold as a going concern and the new owner offers the staff jobs at the same terms, redundancy does not apply. Usually, service with the old employer counts as continuous service in respect of future redundancy payments with the new owner of the business.

Redundancy payments

Redundancy payments are based on a method of computation which takes into account the age of the dismissed employee and the number of years service over two years. No account is taken of service before the age of 18, or over the age of 65 in the case of a man and 60 for a woman.

For each year of service between 18 and 21 the employee is entitled to half a week's pay: between the age of 22 and 44 the entitlement is one week's pay per year of service; and in the case of men between 41 and 64 and woman between 44 and 59, one and a half week's pay for every year of service.

There is a limit to the amount of pay per week taken into consideration, although this figure is reviewed each year by the Department of Employment. There is also a ceiling to the amount which can be claimed under the statutory employment laws, and up to 41% can be claimed back by an employer from the government.

To claim this percentage the employer must have followed the procedure laid down by Parliament. Redundancy pay to an employee must be accompanied by a statement of how it is arrived at, on form RP3 which can be obtained from any office of the Department of Employment.

Failure to supply such a statement can result in the employer being fined and jeopardising his own claim for repayment from the Government.

Other reasons for dismissal

The fifth ground for which an employee can be dismissed fairly is under the head of "other substantial reasons". This can be a legal minefield, for there are no generally accepted definitions of what constitutes a "substantial reason". Claims for unfair dismissal are heard by industrial tribunals who arrive at a decision after hearing all the facts.

Some tribunals have held economic necessity to be a substantial reason; others have held this not to be a sufficient cause for dismissal.

Difficulty can also arise when an employed photographer falls victim of an accident or a long illness, which results in a prolonged absence from work and which leads to eventual dismissal. The question to be answered on occasions such as this is: does the dismissal fall into the category of "other substantial reasons"?

It can be argued that the contract of service between employer and photographer has been frustrated by the photographer's inability to continue in employment. If in these circumstances the photographer seeks to establish before an industrial tribunal that he was unfairly dismissed, the onus is on him to show he would have been fit and capable of resuming work within a reasonable period of time.

Neither can a photographer be dismissed on the grounds of sex, race or trade union activity. A women is entitled to return to work after a period of maternity leave, and is deemed to have been unfairly dismissed if she is not allowed to do so unless there are less than five employees; then the employer can claim it is not reasonably practical to take the woman back.

Industrial tribunals

Claims for unfair dismissal are heard by an industrial tribunal, which is presided over by a trained lawyer sitting with representatives of management and trade unions. If it finds in favour of an employee—which is by no means inevitable—it can award monetary compensation which includes a basic award related to rate of pay and length of employment, with an additional award based on loss suffered as a result of unfair dismissal.

On infrequent occasions an industrial tribunal will order a worker to be reinstated. Often in these circumstances an employer will invariably prefer to pay an additional sum of money, which can range from between 13 and 26 weeks pay, rather than take the employee back.

Wrongful dismissal

Although employees usually bring claims for unfair dismissal to an industrial tribunal, there is a further cause of action open to them if they wish to bring it. This is a claim for wrongful dismissal, which is heard in either the High Court or County Court, and is based on the employer's breach of contract with the employee. The advantage of this type of action as far as the employee is concerned, is that there is no need to have served a qualifying period of employment before bringing the action. However, they are expected to mitigate the loss of employment by finding another situation as soon as possible. A claim for unfair dismissal is not forfeited by bringing a separate claim for wrongful dismissal, but employees are not entitled to enrich themselves over and above what they are legally entitled to by bringing both actions.

CHAPTER FOURTEEN

Working for Yourself

To own one's own business is a laudable ambition, especially in the case of photographers who are in the happy position of being able to earn a living from their hobby. However, it is not as simple as that: having taken the decision to make one's living from one's hobby it is vitally important that key questions are asked and answered correctly at the outset if the business is not to be a disaster.

What type of business?

Firstly, it will be necessary to decide what type of photographic business is to be established. If the photographer has a nose for news and a flair for taking newsworthy and dramatic photographs, he can establish himself as a freelance with very little difficulty.

On the other hand, if the photographer wishes to open a studio from where he will carry out some or all of the many branches of what is known as commercial photography, there are many important considerations to be taken into account.

The photographer who goes into business as a freelance news cameraman needs very little more than the ability to take and sell his photographs. There are two essential items he must bear in the mind at the very outset:

insurance, and the keeping of accurate accounts on which tax will eventually be assessed, and these points will be dealt with later.

If, however, the freelance decides to open an office cum darkroom and employ either secretarial help or another photographer, different factors must be kept in mind.

There are, in fact, three basic types of business a photographer could establish: a one man business, partnership, or limited company. The simplest of these is the one man or sole trader business, but this can have disadvantages, the main one being when it comes to raising any finance which may be necessary to establish or continue the business.

Working on your own

Many such businesses start with very little capital and, indeed, a photographer who has his own equipment has initially little need of capital provided he is assured of sufficient work to bring in money for his needs. The problems arise should the business seek further capital, for either expansion or to tide it over a slack period.

The obvious place to raise capital is one's own bank, which is almost certainly going to require security of some form. If a large loan is required that security may well take the form of a charge on the photographer's house, if he is the owner.

This poses two problems: if the house is being bought on a mortgage, it will be necessary for the building society or any other financial institution which has granted the mortgage, to give its permission for what is known as a second charge to be placed on the house.

Whether or not this permission is necessary, any financial institution which loans a substantial sum of money against the security of a house will not only require the owner—or joint owners if the house is in the name of, for example, the photographer and his wife—to consent to the house being pledged as security, but any other person who has an interest in the equity of the house will also have to consent. In most cases this will be the photographer's spouse if they are not already the joint owners.

A photographer who sets up in business under a name other than his own no longer has to register his business name, but he must be careful that he is not using a name which is either nationally known, or known in the locality in which his business is operating. If he does, there is the possibility of a passing off action.

If a business name is used there is a legal requirement for any letterheads, bills, receipts, etc., to carry the name and permanent address of where the business is run and where all correspondence in connection with the business can be addressed.

There is one other major drawback to running a one man business and that is the risk of the owner being forced into bankruptcy if the business fails. Even if the photographer's house has not been pledged as security against a loan, in the event of bankruptcy creditors can, as a last resort, seize the house and sell it to recover monies owed.

Partnership

Partnerships can also be a source of problems. The Partnership Act 1890 describes a partnership as a relationship which exists between persons carrying on a business in common with a view to profit. If two photographers got together to carry on a business as a photographic news agency, or to open a commercial studio, undoubtedly the law would consider this to be a partnership.

Unless there is agreement to the contrary, the Partnership Act states that all profits must be shared equally, as must losses. Under the Act, individual partners have the right to be paid by the other partners for individual payments made, or liabilities incurred, in the course of running the business.

It is quite possible that an experienced photographer who has built up a flourishing business may wish to take a younger person into partnership. If this is the case and the new partner is not to receive half the profits, it will be necessary for a partnership agreement to be drawn up which will state in what proportion the profits—or losses if they are sustained—are to be split, and who will have the major say in any decisions which may affect the day to day or future running of the business.

Such matters as payment of pension when one partner retires, or whether other persons can be taken into partnership, should also be included in the agreement. At this stage a word of warning must be sounded: photographers going into partnership should not attempt to draw up a partnership agreement on their own. This is a matter of such great importance that the advice of a solicitor should be sought, so that all parties to an agreement are fully aware of each other's responsibilities, rights and share of any profits.

It must also be remembered that partners have a collective responsibility, not only for the running of the business but for any debts incurred, and creditors are entitled to go against the particular partner they think best able to meet their claims. Usually a partner will not be held responsible for debts incurred before he joined the partnership, nor for those after he has ceased to be a partner, although he will he held liable with other partners for those incurred before he left the partnership.

Most partnerships are created for an unlimited period of time but this does not mean that a partner cannot be ousted if there is a genuine reason for the other partner(s) to want him to leave.

There can be written into partnership agreements conditions under which a particular partner can be removed, and in extreme cases a court can order the dissolution of a partnership.

All of the above underlines the need for obtaining legal advice before even the simplest of partnership agreements are entered into.

Setting up a company

The third way of running a business is by creating a limited company, which then has a separate legal entity and is responsible for its own debts. Shareholders are legally liable only to the extent of the shares they hold. Thus if two photographers form a limited company with capital of £5,000 and each have 2,500 £1 shares each, they may well have paid £2,500 into the company at its formation. If the company goes into liquidation— only individuals go bankrupt—the two shareholders have lost their original investment and nothing else. On the other hand, if either or both of the subscribers to the company have taken out 2,500 shares but have only paid 50p a share, they will be liable in the event of the company being wound up, to pay the balance of the money owed on the shares they hold.

A company may be either a private one or a public limited company (PLC), and for the purpose of this book it will be assumed that the photographer wishing to form a company is thinking in terms of a private one. Indeed, a public limited company has to have a minimum capital of

£50,000, and can have its shares available to the public through either the Unlisted Securities Market or a full quotation on the Stock Exchange.

Legal requirements of companies

There are a number of important but not particularly onerous legal formalities which have to be gone through before a company can be formed, and again it is worth seeking advice and help from an accountant and/or solicitor.

The formalities consist of lodging a number of documents with the Registrar of Companies, which for a private company number no more than four.

These are:

The Memorandum of Association;
The Articles of Association;
Statement of the authorised share capital; and,
A statutory declaration that all the requirements of the various Companies Acts have been met.

It is arguable that the two most important of these necessary documents are the Memorandum of Association and the Articles of Association. The Memorandum of Association contains the name of the company and states whether the registered office—which need not be the place from where the business is run—is situated in England and Wales or Scotland.

The Memorandum must also contain the objects of the company. It is advisable for these objects to be as widely drawn as possible. For the photographer who sets up a company to undertake any or all forms of commercial photography, wisdom dictates that he should include in the Memorandum of Association the rights of the company to undertake any ancilliary business associated with photography, such as the selling and processing of films and even photographic equipment and accessories.

The reason for drawing the objects as widely as possible is to enable the company to branch out into fields covered by the objectives should it wish to do so. Unless these future objectives are stated in the Memorandum of Association, they can be held to be *ultra vires*, that is, beyond the powers of the company to undertake such work, and this can result in legal complications.

The Memorandum of Association will also state the amount of share capital and that the liability of members—shareholders—is limited.

The difference between the Memorandum of Association and the Articles of Association is that the latter is what may be termed a domestic document, inasmuch as it determines how shares are to be transferred, the rights of shareholders, how directors may be appointed and removed, when meetings are held and, perhaps the most important, the borrowing powers of the company.

Unless the company has the power to borrow money it is prohibited by law from doing so. Even if the company has borrowing powers, a financial institution will take a commercial view of a request for finance, and if the company's assets are considered to be insufficient to cover the amount of the loan, other security will be required and this could well take the form of a charge on property owned by the directors. If the only tangible asset owned by a director sufficient enough to cover the loan is the director's or directors' houses, the same consideration as far as any other person with an interest in the equity as referred to earlier in this chapter, will apply.

Directorship and income tax

Companies have to have directors, and any private companies which a photographer is likely to set up will probably have the photographer and one other person as a director. These names, together with their shareholding, also have to be notified to the Registrar of Companies. The company also has to have a company secretary, which is usually one of the directors as far as small companies are concerned.

In practice, directors will in all probability be actively engaged in the operation of the company, and should this be the case it is in their own interest to decide whether or not they will take their share of the profits and pay tax on an annual basis, or be employed by the company and take a regular salary, paying tax either weekly or monthly on the PAYE system. Which course a director chooses to take must depend upon his or her own individual circumstances, and before any decision is taken professional advice should be sought.

A limited company must file its annual accounts with the Registrar of Companies each year, and the company secretary has to notify the Registrar of any change of shareholding or of directors and company secretary. These are not onerous duties, and should not deter any photographer from forming his own company.

Employers' obligations

Initially, a small company is unlikely to employ many people, but if it does so it incurs a number of legal responsibilities towards its employees which can be grouped into two convenient heads: not to be unfairly dismissed—which has already been dealt with in the previous chapter—and to work in conditions which do not impair the employee's health and safety.

Unless part time employees or immediate relatives are employed, there is an obligation placed by law on an employer to ensure the health and safety of his employees. Shops have to be registered with the local authority, and this would also cover photographic studios; the law relating to conditions under which employees work is contained in the Offices, Shops & Railway Premises Act 1963, and The Health and Safety at Work Act 1974.

It is not essential to go into great detail as far as these two Acts are concerned; it is sufficient to note that the former does not confine itself simply to the shop or studio, but to all parts of the premises used by the staff, and even to the approaches. Floors and steps have to be cleaned at least once a week, and furniture and fittings also have to be kept in a clean condition. There are also regulations laid down as to the amount of space each member of staff is entitled to, and the minimum temperature which has to be maintained. It is laid down that within an hour of staff commencing work, the temperature must have reached 16° centigrade.

Furthermore, ventilation must be adequate, as must lighting, and a store provided for employees to keep their clothes if they have to change to carry out their duties.

Safety of customers

There are similar obligations imposed by law to provide for the safety of customers, which is contained in The Occupiers Liability Act 1957. This Act imposes on occupiers of premises a common law duty of care to ensure visitors do not come to harm, which in effect means that premises must be reasonably safe for visitors. As far as a photographic shop or studio is concerned, the visitor does not have to be invited in. The law assumes that where premises of this type are concerned, a person who enters them as a potential customer is assumed to have been invited in.

Even tresspassers are entitled to a measure of protection under the Act. Although a trespasser enters premises at his own risk, the occupier is expected to display a common duty of humanity, which means he is not entitled to set traps or other devices which can cause injury.

Furthermore, a higher standard of care is expected to be shown by occupiers towards children who may come onto the premises.

An occupier whose premises are made unsafe—thus resulting in injury caused to a visitor—as a result of work carried out by a contractor, will not be liable if the occupier had taken reasonable care to ensure that the work was carried out by a competent contractor and done properly.

In the case of a photographic studio with its own darkroom in which chemicals are kept which could be harmful, a notice stating this fact and disclaiming responsibility for harm caused to unauthorised visitors would, it is submitted, be reasonable, and one which would be upheld by the courts, if only because there would be no reason for a visitor—unauthorised or otherwise—to enter a darkroom.

CHAPTER FIFTEEN

Loss, Damage and Insurance

It is not inappropriate to end with the subject of insurance, which all photographers be they amateurs, semi or full time professionals, should carry, not only to reimburse themselves for loss, theft or damage to equipment, but to cover themselves against any claims which may be made against them.

Insuring equipment

All photographic equipment should be insured against loss, theft or damage. If such equipment is included in a photographer's house insurance, he should be certain it is also covered for anything which may happen to it when it is being used outside the house. Many household policies do not give cover for individual items when not actually in the house, and it is essential to remember that representatives of insurance companies, employees or agents, cannot be expected to read the mind of a person seeking insurance. If, as commonsense dictates should be the case, expensive equipment is to be insured outside the house, it is essential for the insured person to make certain this is the case.

Premises and vehicles

In the previous chapter the responsibilities of an employer towards his staff and visitors to shop and/or studio was dealt with. Employers are required by law to carry insurance to cover staff against accidents while at work. All the major insurance companies offer a package for a comparatively modest sum, which offers not only this protection on behalf of staff, but also such risks as fire and theft.

What many people who take out insurance fail to realise, with, sometimes, unfortunate results when a claim is repudiated, is that a policy of insurance constitutes a contract between the insurer and the insured.

It is, in fact, rather more than that: a policy of insurance calls for what the law calls *uberrimei fides*, that is utmost faith on the part of the insured to declare any facts which, if known to the insurer, would result in the risk being refused or, if accepted, at a higher premium. For example, if a photographic studio or shop is in an area where there have been a number of break-ins—especially if the shop and/or studio was a victim and no claim was made to the insurance company concerned—these facts must be reported when the premium is renewed, because it is obvious that such knowledge would be likely to affect the premium charged.

The photographer who is most likely to be at risk is the semi-professional, who may have a full time job from Monday to Friday but on Saturday undertakes to photograph weddings for which he needs to use his car. It is most likely that his car is insured for domestic and social use only, which probably includes cover for travelling to and from his place of work.

Such cover is most unlikely to extend to part time, semi-professional photographic work such as taking wedding photographs. Vehicles which are insured for business use are usually subject to a higher premium, because they are on the road more often and therefore the risk of being involved in an accident is that much greater.

The semi-professional photographer who has to dash from wedding to wedding on a Saturday is likely to take risks which would not normally be taken; consequently, the risk is that much higher. It is essential that a photographer in this category should take out additional insurance to cover use of his vehicle for such business.

Damage or loss to photographs

There have been many instances where photographers—professional and amateur—have submitted photographs to newspapers and magazines for publication which have subsequently been lost or damaged.

Obviously it is in the interest of good relations with contributors for newspapers and magazines to take good care of photographs, be they prints, transparencies or negatives, but with the best will in the world there is no foolproof system which can offer one hundred per cent guarantee against loss or damage.

It is not easy to decide categorically what the position of a newspaper or magazine is if photographic material is lost or destroyed. Of course if the photograph has been commissioned and purchased outright by a particular publication then the problem does not arise.

On the other hand if a negative or slide is destroyed or lost so that nothing can replace it, who is to blame? It is arguable that if the photograph was requested as part of a commercial transaction by a particular publication, on the understanding on both sides that it was to be returned, then there can be little doubt that if damage or loss is sustained while in the hands of that publication it is their responsibility. The only argument which may follow is the quantum of damages, and much would depend on the commercial value of the material.

But what if a photograph is submitted on spec to a publication? It is not unreasonable to assume that even in these circumstances a general duty of care is owed by the publication to the photographer or whoever submitted the material, although it is doubtful if any publication would accept liability without some argument.

Insurance of photographs

Finally, there is the question of insuring photographs against loss in the developing and printing process, or when in the hands of publishers. It is of the utmost importance that a photographer who incurs expense to take photographs either for his own pleasure, or for reward, should insure them against loss, because of the difficulties discussed earlier in this book in claiming against a firm of developers and printers. This is also of importance in the case of photographs lost or damaged whilst under consideration by publishers or other clients, where again, claims for damages may be difficult to sustain.

One difficulty the photographer will face is in quantifying the amount the photographs are worth in the commercial market. No problem arises if the photographer has been commissioned, but it will be necessary to take a commercial view of uncommissioned photographs. If the particular photographer has talent and ability which is known to potential publishers, a value can be placed on the photographs, and although this may be open to argument on the part of the insurer should the need to claim arise, there is a recognisable yardstick against which future loss can be measured.

Photographers considering this type of insurance would be well advised to use the services of a reputable insurance broker, who should be able to find a Lloyds underwriter willing to accept the risk, but it cannot be stressed too highly that the exact insurance requirements should be put in writing for the broker.

This is not an unnecessary caveat; it is essential, for if anything should go wrong and the insurance negotiated is not what was needed, the photographer has a case in negligence against the broker, for he (the photographer) was relying on that broker's expertise and knowledge to negotiate the exact type of insurance required.

All in all, insurance can play a major role in the photographer's life, whether he is an amateur or professional, so the importance of getting it right cannot be stressed too much.

Useful Addresses

BUSINESS AND TRADE

British Insurance Brokers' Association
BIBA House, 14 Bevis Marks, London EC3A 7NT. Tel: 01-623 9043.

Association of British Chambers of Commerce
212a Shaftesbury Avenue, London WC2H 8EW. Tel: 01-240 5831.

Companies Registration Office
Crown Way, Maindy, Cardiff CF4 3UZ. Tel: 0222 388588.

Customs & Excise, HM
King's Beam House, Mark Lane, London EC3R 7HE. Tel: 01-626 1515.

Employment, Department of
Caxton House, Tothill Street, London SW1H 9NA. Tel: 01-273 3000.

Health & Social Security, Department of
Alexander Fleming House, Elephant and Castle, London SE1 6BY. Tel: 01-407 5522.

Inland Revenue, Board of
Somerset House, London WC2R 1LB. Tel: 01-438 6622.

National Chamber of Trade
Enterprise House, Pack and Prime Lane, Henley-on-Thames, Oxon RG9 1TU.
Tel: 0491 576161.

Trade & Industry, Department of
1 Victoria Street, London SW1H 0ET. Tel: 01-215 7877.

CONSUMER

Advertising Standards Authority
Brook House, Torrington Place, London WC1E 7HN. Tel: 01-580 5555.

National Consumer Council
20 Grosvenor Gardens, London SW1W 0DH. Tel: 01-730 3469.

Office of Fair Trading
Field House, 15/25 Bream's Buildings, London EC4A 1PR. Tel: 01-242 2858.

Scottish Consumer Council
314 St Vincent Street, Glasgow G3 8XW. Tel: 041-226 5261.

GOVERNMENT & OTHER OFFICIAL BODIES

Central Office of Information
Hercules Road, Westminster Bridge Road, London SE1 7DU. Tel: 01-928 2345.

Defence, Ministry of
Main Building, Whitehall, London SW1A 2HB Tel: 01-218 9000.

Environment, Department of the
2 Marsham Street, London SW1P 3EB. Tel: 01-276 0990.

Home Office
Queen Anne's Gate, London SW1H 9AT. Tel: 01-273 3000.

National Trust
36 Queen Anne's Gate, London SW1H 9AS. Tel: 01-222 9251.

Nature Conservancy Council
Northminster House, Peterborough PE1 1UA. Tel: 0733 40345.

LEGAL

British Copyright Council
Copyright House, 29–33 Berners Street, London W1P 3DB. Tel: 01-580 5544.

Director of Public Prosecutions
4–12 Queen Anne's Gate, London SW1H 9AZ. Tel: 01-213 4268.

Law Officer Department (Attorney General/Solicitor General)
Royal Courts of Justice, Strand, London WC2A 2LL. Tel: 01-936 6000.

The Law Society
113 Chancery Lane, London WC2A 1PL. Tel: 01-242 1222.

The Law Society of Scotland
26 Drumsheugh Gardens, Edinburgh WH3 7YR. Tel: 031-226 7411.

Lord Advocate's Department
Fielden House, 10 Great College Street, London SW1P 3SL. Tel: 01-212 7676.

National Council for Civil Liberties
21 Tabard Street, London SE1 4LA. Tel: 01-403 3888.

Public Records Office (legal records)
Chancery Lane, London WC2A 1LR. Tel: 01-405 0721.

Solicitors Complaints Bureau
Portland House, Stag Place, London SW1E 5BL. Tel: 01-834 2288.

Index